SO-AEC-276

PULPIT GIANTS

PULPIT GIANTS

What Made Them Great

by

DONALD E. DEMARAY

MOODY PRESS

CHICAGO

ISBN: 0-8024-6950-7

9-87

TO

the Reverend Clyde E. VanValin,

warm friend,

skilled pastor,

New Testament preacher

CONTENTS

PREFACE

"I will make my words in thy mouth fire," declared the Lord to Jeremiah; and for him the urgency of preaching was like "a burning fire shut up in my bones" (Jer 5:14; 20:9).

A burning coal touched the lips of Isaiah, and he prophesied.

Every one of the twenty-five pulpit giants in this book was possessed of what one writer in the homiletical field calls "radioactive earnestness." They had a burning in their soul that made it imperative to preach. They spoke out for God with great energy and urgency.

Thus, John Wesley has been called an incendiary; Benjamin Franklin went to hear Whitefield because he could watch a man "burn"; and Paul Rees, who preaches on the fire of the Spirit, is himself a man on fire.

This seems to be the one underlying characteristic of all great preachers: they burn with a holy passion to communicate. If this fact is not always stated per se in the essays that follow, it is always the assumed background.

The pulpit men of this volume come from a variety of settings and centuries. Naturally, the century of religious genius, the eighteenth, is included, but so are the pivotal seventeenth and nineteenth centuries, and others, too. Many denominational backgrounds are represented—Congregational, Methodist, Presbyterian. Several national backgrounds are represented, too, such as Africa, America, England. Christ, who knows no boundaries, was common to all.

Also common to each man was the keen reality of biblical faith and genuine theological liveliness. Each of the pul-

9

pit giants included shines precisely because of his "sheer god-liness." True, each had his distinctive gifts and developed his own vital skills, but the reader quickly will see that every one of them has that special calling and filling of the Spirit of God that set them aflame with a burning in their souls.

And now read on to the men themselves with their exciting explorations, meaningful ministries, and good examples.

FRANCIS ASBURY

Pioneer Preacher

1745-1816

Francis Asbury

From an engraving by A. H. Ritchie, reprinted from *The Pioneer Bishop: or, The Life and Times of Francis Asbury* by W. P. Strickland
(New York: Carlton & Porter, 1858), frontispiece.

FRANCIS ASBURY

FRANCIS ASBURY made an astonishing impact on the New World. He preached sixteen thousand five hundred sermons, rode about six thousand miles per year on horseback, gave leadership to the largest episcopal area in the history of world Methodism, and closed his ministry with over seven hundred traveling preachers, plus more than two thousand local preachers, and well over two hundred thousand members. A tireless preacher of the gospel and an exacting organizer, he drove himself relentlessly.

We call Asbury the Father of American Methodism, yet he was not an American by birth. He came from England as a missionary of Methodism in 1771, and his accomplishments were achieved under the most trying of circumstances. With a salary of only sixty-four dollars per year, the menace of illness and disease, and the almost daily threat to his person, he blazed new trails in uncharted America. He had no place to call his own home and was never married. Wesley, back in England, had appointed him general assistant in America. Then, at the historic Christmas Conference in 1784, Thomas Coke and Francis Asbury were elected as the joint superintendents of the newly founded Methodist Episcopal Church in America.

Francis Asbury had been converted while praying with a companion in his father's barn. He said that, from that moment on, he was "happy, free from guilt and fear, had power over sin, and felt great inward joy." Soon Francis had a Bible study group made up of his friends. Moreover, he was awakened intellectually and developed a habit of continuous reading. He went to hear men of God, such as Fletcher at Wednesbury, proclaim the gospel. He read the literature of such preachers as Whitefield and Cennick. His conversion experience definitely had changed his life.

But Asbury was not content with a single experience with God. "I live in God from moment to moment," he said, and it was this continuing contact with God that provided his continuing motivation for ministry.

Benjamin Gregory, one of Asbury's many biographers, writes, "He was a true Methodist in prayer." Gregory points out that during one period Asbury prayed three hours each morning; at another period he prayed seven times daily; and even when the number of preachers in the Methodist Episcopal Church had grown into the hundreds, "he prayed the most and the best of all men I knew."

Typical of his spirit is this journal entry: "Rose this morning with a determination to fight or die, and spent an hour in earnest prayer. Lord, keep me ever watchful."

When Asbury arrived in America, there were but nine Methodist preachers, yet he was not one to yield to the frustration of circumstances. He preached at the beginning of the day, sometimes as early as 5:00 A.M., and before retiring at night. Asbury seldom preached less than an hour. He preached wherever he could—in jails, houses, schools, at riversides, in bars. " 'I preached' is his *Journal*'s most typical entry," says L. C. Rudolph. He was in fact a tireless itinerant. He preached everywhere. As Rudolph puts it, "He preached wherever his horse stopped!" Excerpts from his journals will illustrate his wholehearted dedication to the work of a traveling preacher:

> After preaching at H's in the morning, I intended preaching in the schoolhouse in the evening: but it would not contain half the people, so I stood at the door and the people without.

> This evening I had a very solemn family meeting, and spoke separately and privately to every one, both black and white.

Unexpectedly found the people at two o'clock waiting to hear the Word. I preached with liberty, and the power of God was felt in the hearts of many.

Preached at James Pressbury's to many people who could feel the Word, and with much power in my own soul. Then rode three miles into the Neck, and had a solemn and heart-affecting time preaching from Revelation 2:11.

Went about five miles to preach in our first preaching house. The house had no windows or doors, the weather was cold, so that my heart pitied the people when I saw them so exposed. Putting a handkerchief over my head, I preached, and after an hour's intermission, the people waiting all the time in the cold, I preached again.

Like all preachers then and now, he had his bad moments: "Losing some of my ideas in preaching," he wrote in his journal, "I was ashamed of myself, and pained to see the people waiting to hear what the blunderer had to say. May these things humble me, and show me where my strength lieth!" But one who had heard him over fifteen hundred times said he demonstrated rich variety and preached impressively.

Yes, he was a typical itinerant of early American Methodism. He was rough, ready, simple, and plain. That is why he enjoyed the preaching of a Brother Cromwell who possessed an unaffected simplicity.

His journal for November 22, 1779, is the perfect summary of this man's remarkable life. He says he rose between four and five, spent an hour in prayer and meditation, then read some chapters from the Bible before daylight. "I want to be all devoted to God; every moment given up to Christ." Then he says he rode to Maxfield's where he preached to perhaps three hundred on the text, "Lord, are there few that be saved?" He showed what we are saved from, how we are saved, and why there are few saved. He proclaimed that no unrepentant sinner, no "violent sectarian," no hypocrites or backsliders, not even those who are only casual seekers can be saved.

During his last days, he had to be carried into churches to preach the gospel. Though feeble, he did the best he could. His last sermon was in Richmond, Virginia, in March of 1816. The last day of that month he went to his eternal reward.

* * *

The interested reader will want to see L. C. Rudolph's biography, *Francis Asbury* (Nashville: Abingdon, 1966). Rudolph includes a bibliography.

There is a 1958 printing of *Journal and Letters of Francis Asbury* in three volumes, edited by Elmer T. Clark, J. Manning Potts, and Jacob S. Payton (Nashville: Abingdon).

AUGUSTINE OF HIPPO
Homiletical Preacher
354-430

Augustine

From a fresco in the Lateran Library, circa 600, reprinted from *Augustine the Bishop by F. Van Der Meer,* translated by B. Battershaw and G. R. Lamb (New York: Sheed & Ward, 1961), facing page 216. Used by permission.

AUGUSTINE OF HIPPO

A HOMILETICAL GENIUS, Augustine had a nearly perfect sense of sermon construction and communication. Evidence for that is Book IV of his *Christian Doctrine,* a textbook for men training for the ministry. Further evidence is the enthusiastic response of his hearers.

His genius is the more amazing when it is remembered that Augustine was a pioneer in other fields, too. As a forerunner in the psychology of religion, we still look to his analysis of human pride. As a foundation thinker in theology, we are still intrigued by his analysis of the Trinity and of many other doctrines. We stand in awe of his ability as an original writer to reduce abstract concepts to paper. But we must look at his background to understand this fascinating man.

In the youthful Augustine we see a strange mixture of sensuousness, intellectualism, cultism, and piety. For many years he had a concubine; from his youth he showed signs of serious academic exploration; for nine years he was a member of a cultic movement known as Manichaeism; but he could never completely escape the influence of his godly mother, Monica, whose prayers were ultimately the cause of his conversion.

His conversion took place in Milan, Italy, where he had gone to teach rhetoric in A.D. 384. In this city he listened to the compelling preaching of Ambrose. At first, Augustine was interested only in Ambrose's rhetorical skills and went to hear him as an academic exercise, but he began to ponder the preacher's message. At the same time, a deepened awareness of his helpless, sinful condition brought to him a sense of desperation. This feeling of hopelessness erupted into a crisis of conversion, the account of which is classic. Rushing into

19

a garden, he heard the voice of a child from next door say, "Take up and read." He opened to a copy of the epistles he had been perusing. His eyes fell on Romans 13:13-14: "Not in rioting and drunkenness, not in chambering and wantonness, not in strife and envying. But put ye on the Lord Jesus Christ, and make not provision for the flesh, to fulfil the lusts thereof." With the reading of those lines came the moment of conversion. He was radically changed! From then on, he had the power to resist temptation and possessed an inner composure he heretofore had not known.

This conversion experience took place in late summer, A.D. 386. He was baptized in the Easter season of 387. Augustine's *Confessions,* a devotional classic, is the autobiographical source of information about his spiritual pilgrimage.

In due course, he returned to his native Africa and spent the greater part of his life in the port city of Hippo, a Roman municipality of perhaps thirty thousand. He did not seek ordination; indeed, it was thrust upon him by the people. He preferred the quiet life of a scholar and searcher after God, but he became a powerful preacher of the gospel and gave himself to his simple and uneducated parishioners. They loved him because he spoke to them in private as well as in public. His people came to him about their most trivial decisions and daily experiences.

There were several factors that contributed to Augustine's homiletical genius. He had a great mind. For years he secluded himself to work out a philosophy of life. Beyond that, he had gone through the throes of rugged human experience and thus possessed an empathy with other people which they could sense. If his rhetorical knowledge gave him the theory of public speaking, his experiential knowledge gave him a workable program of human communication. Insight into speaker-audience relationships was perfected by his power to apply that insight.

It is said that divine love was the central theme of Augustine's preaching. He knew from experience the reality of that love, and his people could sense that he had known despair and been rescued from it by the touch of God's Spirit. That, after all, is really what makes people listen to a preacher —that, plus the skill to make contact with an audience.

Augustine was a careful expositor of the Word of God. He taught the Scriptures "sentence by sentence, often word by word," someone has observed. He consistently gave his people Bible truth and conceived of his position in the pulpit as that of a teacher as well as a preacher. The writings of John and Paul, and the Psalms were favorites with him. With his conscientious exposition came the inevitable emphasis on ethics. Drunkenness, sexual sins, telling untruths, theft—all these and more were the objects of his eloquent censure.

The saint of Hippo had a talent for communication. He knew, for example, the wisdom of being brief. Sometimes, gauging his audience's attention span, he spoke for only ten minutes. He was, moreover, a creative preacher. Once, when an assistant read the wrong psalm, he composed a new sermon on the spot. He knew, too, the high importance of freedom in the pulpit. He stressed that an address prepared beforehand and delivered from memory limited the speaker's ability to communicate effectively because he could not respond to the reactions of his listeners. An attentive crowd will show if the speaker is understood; and if he is not, the sensitive speaker will rephrase what he has said until the crowd responds.

Food, said Augustine, is analogous to the preaching message in this way: "The very food without which it is impossible to live must be flavored to meet the tastes of the majority." To him mere words and eloquence were unimportant in themselves; truth was all important. But truth must be served in a tasty and digestible form—that was his rule.

Augustine was outspoken about preachers living consistent Christian lives before their parishioners. A man may be wicked but speak the truth; he may even speak the truth eloquently. But he will help more people if he himself is good. If the congregation sees that the preacher does not act in accordance with the standards he teaches his people, they will cease to listen with submission. In despising the preacher, Augustine warned, they will come to despise the Word.

Finally, observe the saintliness of Augustine. The man who utters sacred things must enter the pulpit in an attitude of prayer. "Who can make us say what we ought, and in the way we ought, except Him in whose hand both we and our speeches are?" He believed the Holy Spirit Himself speaks through the prayerful preacher to the open hearer.

* * *

Book IV of Augustine's *Christian Doctrine,* the first homiletics text book, is obtainable in paperback—a 1958 edition, translated with an introduction by D. W. Robertson and published by the Bobbs-Merrill Company of Indianapolis.

BAXTER OF KIDDERMINSTER
Urgent Preacher
1615-1691

Richard Baxter

From a painting by Robert Walker, reprinted from *A Life of the Rev. Richard Baxter, 1615-1691* by F. J. Powicke (New York: Houghton Mifflin, 1924). Used by permission. Photograph by Henry James.

BAXTER OF KIDDERMINSTER

"There have been three or four parishes in England which have been raised, by their pastors, to a national, almost world-wide fame," said Dean Stanley. "Of these the most conspicuous is Kidderminster."

Kidderminster is a country town in the Severn Valley of England. Its parish church is very old; it was old even when Richard Baxter came there as minister in 1641. But who had heard of Kidderminster before Baxter?

Baxter made Kidderminster famous, but it was illness that made Richard Baxter great. We should say illnesses, for he had many diseases. More than two dozen doctors treated him, but none gave him hope; indeed, he was told he could die at any time. "For years," said Ezra S. Tipple, one of Baxter's biographers, "he entered the pulpit in the fear that he might not leave it alive."

Richard Baxter looked upon his affliction as "an invaluable mercy" because he learned it weakened temptation, kept him from valuing the world too highly, and taught him the importance of every moment of time. Probably the best-known lesson he has shared with us, however, is the necessity of preaching vital truth to sinners with compassion—"as a dying man to dying men!"

It was this sense of urgency that motivated Richard Baxter to set in motion a pastoral program of remarkable variety and vitality. Catechizing, which he said was as difficult a task as preaching, paid off in the conversion and nurture of youth to such an extent that he could say that his best success was with the young people. Yet he neglected no one. He called from house to house and put into practice the high level of pastoral care of individuals which he outlines in *The Reformed Pastor*.

Soon the Kidderminster parish church was too small. One balcony was erected, then another and another until five were constructed and the church could hold no more.

Prior to his illnesses, Baxter confessed, he never once thought of putting anything into print. But then, with a new awareness of time, he began to write. What an immense amount of material he published—over a hundred and fifty separate pieces of literature from pamphlets to very long books. One of his biographers, Orme, has shown by comparison the extent of his works: Bishop Hall's works amounted to ten volumes; Lightfoot's, thirteen volumes; Jeremy Taylor's, fifteen; Dr. Goodwin's, about twenty; Dr. Owen's, twenty-eight. Baxter's works, if printed in a uniform edition, would come to sixty volumes.

Three volumes are possibly his best known. *The Saints' Everlasting Rest* was written after he heard the physicians declare the imminent possibility of his death. *The Call to the Unconverted,* which Francis Asbury said was "one of the best pieces of human composition in the world to awaken the lethargic souls of poor sinners," was used to convert so remarkable a number that Baxter could say, "Through God's mercy I have had information of almost whole households converted by this small book." *The Reformed Pastor* forms a part of the classic literature on the pastor's task, and Philip Doddridge said it ought to be read by every young minister before going into the pastorate.

"What have we our time and strength for, but to lay both out for God? What is a candle made for, but to be burnt?" That was Richard Baxter's philosophy of time and work. Thus it was with all diligence that he prepared his sermons and himself for preaching. God blessed his pulpit work at Kidderminster. On Sunday, all was peaceful and quiet. As one passed by homes, families could be heard singing hymns and reading sermons. When he first came to the country village, about one family in each street came to worship; when he left in 1660, all of the families on some streets were alive to God! There were even some bartenders' families who had been converted to Christ.

Someone said of his preaching that he talked "about another world like one that had been there." He spoke "with great vivacity and freedom, and his thought had a peculiar edge."

What gave this peculiar edge to his preaching? First, he himself was alive to God. He did not ask his people to be something he was not.

Then, there was about him a holy earnestness. We may not agree with his viewpoint that one should be all seriousness in the pulpit, but great earnestness is commendable and necessary. People knew he meant business.

Third, he gave attention to as mechanical a matter as voice projection. Few speak up loudly, he said, and most who do have no content to speak up about.

Fourth, he absolutely refused to be dull. "What! Speak coldly for God and for men's salvation? Can we believe that our people must be converted or condemned and yet we speak in a drowsy tone? In the name of God, brethren, labor to awaken your hearts before you get to the pulpit, that you may be fit to waken the hearts of sinners."

Fifth, Baxter was a careful and enthusiastic student.

His sixth asset was his refusal to speak in an affected manner. "The want of a familiar tone and expression is as great a defect in most of our deliveries as anything whatsoever, and that which we should be very careful to amend. When a man hath a reading or a declaiming tone, few are moved with anything that he saith."

Seventh, the preacher must employ both scripture and reason. "A sermon full of mere words, how neatly soever it be composed, while there is wanting the light of evidence and the life of zeal, is but an image or a well-dressed carcass."

Finally, Baxter was a man of prayer. He got his sermons

on his knees. It is no wonder someone said he had an "extraordinary reliance upon the efficacy of prayer."

* * *

Richard Baxter's *Reformed Pastor*, though a seventeenth century work, provides solid advice on preaching and related work. The Hugh Martin edition is done by S.C.M. Press of London (1956).

For a biography of Richard Baxter, read of him in Ezra S. Tipple's *Some Famous Country Parishes* published in 1911 by Eaton and Mains, New York.

PHILLIPS BROOKS
Boston Preacher

1835-1893

Phillips Brooks

From a portrait by H. G. Smith, reprinted from *Life and Letters of Phillips Brooks* by Alexander V. G. Allen (New York: Dutton, 1900), frontispiece.

PHILLIPS BROOKS

PHILLIPS BROOKS lived at the same time as Dwight Lyman Moody. He was born only two years before and died half a dozen years prior to Moody. They also had a geography in common, both living in Massachusetts during the early and later parts of their lives. But their gifts and callings were very different. Moody was an uneducated shoe salesman, never ordained; Brooks was a Harvard graduate who died as an Episcopal bishop. One used homey illustrations and simple words to communicate the gospel; the other took into the pulpit twenty pages of manuscript tightly packed with insights and information couched in magnificent English. One reached the masses in travels across our country; the other touched the intellectuals of Boston and could preach in Westminster Abbey, London.

Born at the time of the Unitarian-orthodox debate, Phillips was baptized in a Unitarian Church. His mother, however, eventually became dissatisfied with the lack of religious content in Unitarianism; and when Phillips was four, the family joined the Episcopal Church, with the exception of his father, who was confirmed later. It is significant that Phillips Brooks, coming out of this background, was to become God's instrument for restoring respect to evangelical Christianity in Unitarian Boston.

A good deal of the credit for Phillips' success goes to his mother, who has been compared to Susannah Wesley because of the conscientious way she reared her children. Four of her six sons went into the ministry. And it is no wonder! She herself was deeply religious and reflected her convictions in the family's religious routine. Before supper a chapter from the Old Testament was read, which was followed by prayer; then

31

a verse from the gospels was recited by the boys in unison. At night, Mrs. Brooks tucked each child into bed, and to each she told an Old Testament story.

During the religious exercises of the day, the family sang hymns, and the boys were required to memorize a hymn each Sunday and to repeat it at family worship the next night. By the time Phillips Brooks went to Harvard, he had memorized two hundred hymns. It is no wonder that he often wrote hymns and poetry for his own sermons.

Mrs. Brooks faithfully attended a weekly Bible class at the church and then taught the material to her children. William Newton Clarke said she was diligent in Bible study and untiring in her task of teaching it at home.

Brooks attended the famous Boston Latin School and upon graduation from college returned to teach for a year. But he considered his experience there an utter failure, for he had no gift for order and discipline. That sense of failure nearly crushed him. But thanks to patient and careful advice from his father and his pastor, he decided to enter seminary to prepare for the ministry.

His college career was characterized by its excellence. He went to Harvard when James Walker was the president, and on the faculty were such distinguished men as James Russell Lowell, Oliver Wendell Holmes, Henry Wadsworth Longfellow, and Louis John Rudolph Agassiz, the naturalist. Witness to the fact that he took full advantage of available professional guidance was his graduation with honors in 1855.

At Virginia Theological Seminary he went beyond the guidance of teachers and became a distinguished, independent scholar. The Scriptures, the classics, and the scholars he usually read in the original Greek, Hebrew, Latin, German, and French. Said a classmate, "As a classical scholar none matched him. The Greek of the New Testament, as he dealt with it, 'rejoiced like Enoch at being translated.'"

Upon being graduated from seminary he was ordained, and

his first charge was the Church of the Advent in Philadelphia, where he stayed for three years. Next, he was rector of Holy Trinity in the same city. Then in 1869, he returned to the city of his birth, Boston, and to Trinity Church which he rebuilt and where he became so distinguished an orator that it is said when he died, the nation had not mourned a death so much since the decease of President Lincoln. In 1891, just two years before his death, he was elected Bishop of Massachusetts, and people of all denominations hailed this as a great move.

Brooks' pulpit success was due to a variety of factors. First and foremost, he had a sound philosophy of preaching. In what some have said are the best of the Yale Lectures on preaching (1877), he defined preaching as "truth through personality." Truth is based in Jesus Christ, and preaching is really living the Christ-like life and then talking about it on Sunday.

Tall, erect, and poised, he cut a commanding figure in the pulpit. People, it is said, came to Boston not only to hear Brooks but also to see him. Emitting from this man in his pulpit was the Spirit of Christ in such measure that the students at Harvard and the people of Boston were touched and changed for the good. Truth had come through a personality.

Phillips Brooks loved people, and clearly this is another reason for his pulpit success. In a ministerial discussion on parish visitation, and after much talk, he rose to say, "I would like to do nothing but make pastoral calls and meet the people. Indeed, if I did not, I could not preach." He spent every afternoon calling. And he did not ignore the children in his visits; indeed, he loved them very much. It is said that he had a certain childlike quality about him that drew people of all ages. He wrote his famous Christmas carol, "O Little Town of Bethlehem," for his Sunday school. What would one give to be transported back into history to see and hear those children sing it for the first time!

Brooks, always a bachelor, felt keenly the lack of children

in his own home and kept dolls for his brother's children to play with when they came for a visit. In 1890, he wrote to a little blind girl about the love of Jesus and invited her to receive that love into her own heart. That girl was Helen Keller.

Before Trinity Church in Boston stands a statue of Brooks— tall, erect, commanding. Behind him is another statue, that of the Christ. He is slightly higher, and His hand is placed upon the shoulder of Phillips Brooks. The touch of that hand was felt throughout his ministry. It is no wonder that he was a pulpit giant.

* * *

Given at Yale in 1877 when Brooks was forty-two, his published lectures on preaching rank him one of the few homiletical geniuses of all time. A 1964 printing, titled *Phillips Brooks on Preaching,* with an introduction by Theodore Parker Ferris, was done by Seabury Press of New York in the United States and by S.P.C.K. of London in 1965.

JOHN BUNYAN
Imaginative Preacher
1628-1688

John Bunyan

From an engraving by A. H. Ritchie, after a drawing from the life by R. White, preserved in the British Museum, reprinted from *The Life, Times, and Characteristics of John Bunyan* by Robert Philip (New Haven: Mansfield, 1855), frontispiece.

JOHN BUNYAN

THE ENGLISH TOWNS of Bedford and Olney are in close proximity, and both are about fifty miles from London. The Bedford-Olney district is famous for four men. The first is John Newton, writer of "Amazing Grace," counselor, evangelical preacher, head of the Evangelical Party of the Church of England in the eighteenth century, pastor at Olney. The second is Newton's friend William Cowper, the poet of the Evangelical Revival and, as a poet, a voice against slavery. Together Newton and Cowper published *The Olney Hymns*, a well-known and widely used evangelical hymn book. The third is John Howard, a resident of Bedford, who was stirred by John Wesley's preaching and became the father of prison reform. Today there is a statue of Howard in Bedford.

The fourth man lived in the century preceding the other three. He had a passion for preaching, and his sermonizing was characterized by imagination. His pictorial works, the most famous of which is *Pilgrim's Progress*, won him a permanent and notable place in literature. He was, of course, John Bunyan.

John had no famous heritage. His father was a tinker, and of his mother, Margaret Bentley, little is known. But even though his parents were humble, they were of good Bedfordshire stock; and they were careful to provide John an education in the Bedford schools. After his schooling, John became a tinker like his father.

A stint in the army, followed by a return to his trade and marriage to a fine young lady, tell the story of the next page of his life—except for one thing: he was, according to his own testimony, a cursing, lying, blaspheming sinner. From this sinful state the Spirit of God awakened him through a conversation he overheard among a group of women. They were talking about the new birth. Suddenly he wanted information about God and began to seek Him in earnest. But before he experienced the new birth, he went through a fierce struggle, feeling he had sinned far too much ever to be forgiven. He suffered, too, from guilt feelings about his wasted youth. He wondered if he were actually elected.

God used three vehicles to bring John Bunyan out of the doldrums of temptation and into the light of saving grace: his kindly pastor, John Gifford; Luther's *Commentary on Galatians* (the copy he used was so old he was afraid to turn the leaves for fear they would break off) ; and the Scriptures, especially the Song of Solomon. When conversion finally came, he scarcely could lie in bed that night; he felt he must share what had happened. It is no surprise, then, that in due course, Bunyan began to preach. "Some of the most able of the saints," he comments, asked him to speak in church. Preaching frightened him at first; after all, he had little learning. But seeing people helped by clear Bible preaching gave him the courage and stimulus to go on.

Of his sincerity in the pulpit there can be no doubt. He testified that he preached what he felt even when his own soul was convicted by his subject. People came by the hundreds from miles around to hear his unvarnished and genuine proclamation of the gospel. But the Anglican divines were soon jealous, and John Bunyan was put into jail.

What made him a great and helpful preacher? Bible knowledge, experience with God, the sense of a divine call, continuing divine guidance, understanding of human nature, and the ability to put all this into plain and picturesque language—these factors must have been key reasons for Bunyan's pulpit effectiveness. But there was another reason. Contributing considerably to making him a good preacher was his imprisonment. In prison his knowledge of the Bible and the human heart was deepened. November 12, 1660, saw Bunyan arrested for preaching without a license. He could have escaped arrest if he had run away or stopped preaching, but he refused to do either. He chose instead to continue even if it meant suffering rather than violate his faith and principles.

His wife pleaded with the judge to release him because she had four small children to support, one of which was blind. She was forced to rely on charity because the judge would not relent. Instead, he became angry with her. He could not understand why John Bunyan would not change his views if he wanted release.

The imprisoned Bunyan used his time to good advantage. He made long lace tags to support his family; he talked with a great many people who knew his worth as counselor; he preached right from his cell to fellow prisoners and to those who came to hear him; and he studied the Bible. (It might be better to say he mastered it. In one of his works alone there are well over four hundred references to Scripture.) He also did some writing in prison. At times he was free to leave his cell, at other times he was forced to stay confined, but he was in and out of prison for many years. In all this he was attending the school of suffering, and in it he learned intimately the inner workings of the human heart. These he interpreted in the light of Holy Scripture, and he couched his insights in the imaginative language of *Pilgrim's Progress*, a book that has sold more than any other, aside from the Bible itself, in the Christian world. It was John Bunyan's ability to draw accurate and spiritually sensitive word pictures about life that made him the great preacher and writer he was.

What added to the power of his word pictures was his genius for identification with people. He was on the side of the people, and that was immediately clear. To this day, the masses relate to his writings. The very fact that he was Baptist, rather than of the Church of England in the seventeenth century, suggests where his sympathies lay. More, his capacity to picture spiritual conflict with drama and vigorous faith made his writing timeless and realistic. It is no surprise that Londoners flocked to hear John Bunyan and that he was nicknamed "Bishop" Bunyan.

What made Bunyan the communication genius that he was? Six qualities stand out: Bible mastery, an experience with God, a sure sense of divine call and guidance, extraordinary insight into human nature, the mastery of words, and his narrative ability in depicting spiritual conflict and vigorous faith in word pictures.

*   *   *

The *Pilgrim's Progress,* ranking second only to the Bible in popularity, continues to go through many editions. It demonstrates Bunyan's genius for painting pictures with words.

SAMUEL CHADWICK

Compassionate Preacher

1860-1932

Samuel Chadwick

From a photograph owned by R. G. Turnbull. Photograph by
Henry James.

SAMUEL CHADWICK

"WHAT A TIME WE HAD!" wrote Samuel Chadwick of his Clydebank, Birmingham days. "Conversions began the first Sunday." That was typical. Everywhere Chadwick went, people were converted to Christ.

His first assignment, after three years of study at Didsbury College, Manchester, England, was to serve as assistant to the Rev. John Martin in Edinburgh. Revival came and he found himself giving pastoral care to the young Christians.

Clydebank was his next charge. "There was adventure in every venture," said Chadwick. He began preaching out-of-doors, saw drunks saved, fought the influence of the pubs, redeemed women as well as men. He preached twice every Sunday and presented Bible studies in the afternoon in a church crowded with men.

Thirty years later he went back to Clydebank to see his converts. They were still very much alive to God! More, their children were in the church. He asserted that the rewards received by a soul-winner are incalculable.

The Clydebank experience was of three years duration, and at the end of that period he could say that his church was staffed primarily by one-time alcoholics and exbartenders.

His third charge was Leeds. "What a time we had! . . . The revival began on the first Sunday and by the end of September the chapel was full half-an-hour before the time to begin, and police regulated the crowd. Wesley, Leeds, was my jolliest ministry, and the Church was the merriest and saintliest I have ever known."

After Wesley Chapel, Leeds, Chadwick spent a single year at Shoreditch as assistant to Herbert M. Nield. But he returned to Leeds, the town he had come to love so dearly—

this time to Oxford Place Chapel. He filled the coliseum there with three thousand during two or three winters. Conversions took place almost every Sunday in or out of the chapel. Chadwick claimed there was hardly a room in his house in which someone had not accepted Christ.

He had his converts meet in classes; and before he left Leeds, about two thousand people were meeting in groups. Whole classes were organized for converted alcoholics. Street urchins were saved; some were to become preachers.

Mrs. Chadwick developed a team of deaconesses. She got into the homes of the poor, loved them, and showed them the care of Christ.

Up and down the length of Britain went Sam Chadwick, preaching the eternal gospel with a flame burning in his heart. He saw people converted everywhere.

The great secret of his ministry was the Holy Spirit. This is why he said that Whitsuntide (Pentecost) meant more to him than any other festival of the church year.

Five years before he had experienced the filling of the Spirit, he was introduced to William Arthur's *Tongue of Fire*, a book which awakened an interest in him that was never to die. When, at last, he did experience the filling of the Holy Spirit, he was seeking for something else.

He was, with others, seeking revival for a local church where he had been appointed as a lay evangelist. He had preached through fifteen sermons, but there was no quickening. Finally, a dozen people covenanted together. They prayed daily for awakening and met weekly for group prayer. Praying for others, they themselves were brought one by one under a profound sense of weakness. Chadwick experienced an inner conflict that went on for weeks—not over clearly sinful things as one might suppose, but over holy things. Finally he realized that God must be in control of everything. Then came surrender which brought him a realization of Christ's full salvation, a fresh vision of the Almighty, and a heart-felt yearning to see people saved. By the next day God had given him the joy of leading seven people to Christ. Peace, joy, and power were now his through the Spirit.

This was, however, only the beginning of his deeper relationship with the Spirit of God; many subsequent fillings were to come. One such was pivotal. Reading about Gideon and how the Spirit of the Lord came upon him, Chadwick studied the marginal rendering: "The Spirit of the Lord clothed itself with Gideon." "My eyes were opened, and I knew," he explained. "With great daring I crossed out Gideon's name and put in my own."

The filling of the Spirit literally transformed Samuel Chadwick. Now there was a new victory; a new, unexpected intellectual alertness; a new eagerness to explore the truths of the Bible; a new meaning in prayer; a new faith with eyes; a new love which burst into flame; a new appreciation of God and of the living Christ.

No wonder that his preaching became more powerful and hundreds were converted. He testified that Pentecost taught him all he knew about evangelism and that the meaning of the church as the body of Christ was made clear. He learned to raise money without the help of "vanity fair." Also, he was saved from fear of attacks on God's Word, the Christian faith, and the kingdom.

"The Holy Ghost has been the key to my thinking, the defence of my faith, the inspiration of my life, and the effective power in all my work," was his testimony toward the close of his ministry.

With the coming of the Spirit came that compassion which the Lord manifested in His earthly ministry. Chadwick was concerned with the troubled, perplexed people about him in need of the compassion that the Holy Spirit gives. He determined that at the end of his life he would not lament, as had Dr. R. W. Dale, "that he had been more interested in truth than in people."

Samuel Chadwick was a man of the Bible, a man of prayer, a man of education (he was principal of a Methodist college) , a man of the pulpit, but especially a man of compassion who simply had to see people redeemed from their miserable and sinful circumstances.

*   *   *

One of the rich sources of information about Samuel Chadwick is *The Testament of Samuel Chadwick, 1860-1932* (compiled by D. W. Lambert and published by the Epworth Press of London, 1957) , from which the quotations in this chapter were taken.

Another good source is Norman G. Dunning, *Samuel Chadwick* (London: Hodder and Stoughton, 1933) .

ADAM CLARKE
Knowledgeable Preacher
1762?-1832

Adam Clarke

From an engraving by Cochran reprinted from *The Life of the Rev. Adam Clarke, LL.D.*, by J. W. Etheridge (London: Mason, 1859), frontispiece.

ADAM CLARKE

ALMOST EVERYONE KNOWS Adam Clarke as the author of the famous commentary that bears his name. Few know him as a powerful preacher.

It all started in a barn with his conversion. Yes, a Methodist preacher, speaking in a barn, made the gospel invitation so real to young Adam Clarke that he simply couldn't ignore it.

The preacher presented the invitation by describing Christ knocking at his heart's door. Adam let Him in, and from that moment there was a burning in his soul to spread the gospel. That fire glowed brightly for over fifty years.

The fire took him down the roads of his native Ireland. He walked every direction, like John the Baptist, crying to the people to repent. On Sundays he would visit nine or ten villages, preaching in every one.

John Wesley heard of this young and enthusiastic evangelist. Their meeting in England is classic.

"Is it your desire to devote yourself entirely to the work of the Lord?" Wesley asked.

"Sir, I want to do and be what God pleases," Clarke replied eagerly.

"We want a pastor for Bradford circuit," Wesley told the earnest young man. "Hold yourself in readiness to go."

With that, Wesley laid his hands on Adam's head and invoked God's blessing on his ministry. Adam Clarke always considered that his ordination.

God answered Wesley's prayer for an effective ministry for Clarke. At Bradford, revival broke out in less than a year. At St. Austell in Cornwall, despite wretched economic circumstances (rarely more than a meal a day in one year), he had a

49

remarkably fruitful ministry. Revival came everywhere, in crowded chapels and outdoor meetings.

What was the secret of his preaching power? When he preached, he presented a wealth of evangelical truth. It was observed by one who heard him that, as he reached the end of his sermon, he drew together all the truths to which he had previously referred, stressed their importance, and then swept his hands in a broad gesture as though he were sowing grain saying, "There, take these glorious truths—"

The effect on the audience was marvelous. A burst of joy rose up from the crowd.

Independent and fearless, no homiletical custom held Adam Clarke in bondage. He rarely announced divisions in his sermons, and he avoided the customary three main points and a conclusion. Some may have even thought him unorganized until the recapitulation of his ideas at the end. Then it was clear enough that he knew all along where he was going. Actually, he was a brilliant pulpit apologist who took carefully considered arguments along intricate trails. But like a seasoned lawyer, he came out on solid ground.

The eminent biblical preacher of Methodism knew the Bible from beginning to end and had it at his fingertips. His commentary, the product of better than thirty years of arduous work, is representative of his Bible knowledge.

Someone has observed that Adam Clarke took general truth and showed how it was part of the great and harmonious whole of Christian revelation. In turn, that truth, seen in its full context, was beautifully applied to individual needs. No wonder his hearers left comforted!

His preparation was both general and specific. A voracious reader with an insatiable thirst for knowledge, he was always working on general preparation. Nor did he neglect specific preparation, but he was never word or phrase oriented. It was the thought that was important.

Clarke's voice was clear and strong; and he was capable of

forceful projection, most particularly in his conclusion at the point of climax. His Ulster-Scot accent must have added to his powers of communication. Clarke's bodily action was natural. It was not always graceful, but it was always communicative. A great shock of hair—red in youth, white in old age—added to his impressiveness.

Behind this impressive preacher was a life as eloquent as the sermons he delivered. Generous in every way, his heart went out to all, especially the needy. When distance or illness kept him away from his people, he had his wife make his pastoral rounds. "I know you will not let poor Mrs. Fox be neglected," he wrote his wife on one occasion. "While she lives, send her something with my blessing every day." He was courteous in small as well as large things, Robert A. West, author and contemporary, observed.

And with it all, he was an indefatigable worker. He translated the Bible in toto and had equipped himself for that task by learning Greek, Latin, Hebrew, Chaldee, Syriac, French, and nearly all of the modern languages of Western Europe. He did missionary work in many places, including the Channel Islands. In London, during a three-year period, he actually walked seven thousand miles as he went from church to church. At St. Austell, demands on him were unbelievable. He was popular from the moment he started and was sometimes forced to climb into his chapel through the windows, moving as best he could over the seats to the pulpit. It is no wonder that at St. Austell he was forced to preach out-of-doors weekly to those who could not possibly get into the chapel. As one authority says, "He held them spellbound by his word under pelting rains and on deep snow."

Constantly there were additions to the church. A notable addition was Samuel Drew, brought into the church from a shoemaker's bench. He later became a distinguished author and professor at London University. Eventually, Drew shared his speaking talents as a Methodist local preacher.

Clarke's sermons were published in three volumes, and he preached literally thousands of times. No doubt the diligence and intensity of his work load, self-assigned, is to be blamed for keeping him from working on his commentary for a two-year period.

But little held him down. Looking back over his better than fifty years of ministry, he had served as a pastor, conference superintendent, missionary, writer, and commentator.

While attending a conference in Liverpool, he contracted an incurable disease and died before he could reach home. But through the years he had reached home in many a heart from the pulpit.

*   *   *

Preachers may be interested in a chapter on Clarke the preacher in J. W. Etheridge's *The Life of the Rev. Adam Clarke* (New York: Carlton and Porter, 1858).

JONATHAN EDWARDS
Thoughtful Preacher
1703-1758

Jonathan Edwards

From an old print.

JONATHAN EDWARDS

JOHN WESLEY was but five months old when Jonathan Edwards was born in October of 1703. Jonathan was one of eleven children; the others were all girls. The atmosphere of his home was characterized by its strict discipline in religion and morals, honest labor, and thrift. Timothy Edwards, his father, led the way in discipline. As a youth, Mr. Edwards received two Harvard degrees, B.A. and M.A., in a single year. In the pastorate, he ministered to the same church, Windsor, Connecticut Congregational, for some sixty years.

Jonathan assumed the same disciplined stance as his father. Before he was nineteen, he had written out some seventy resolutions which he kept religiously. The following reflects his steel character: "Resolved: That every man should live to the glory of God. Resolved Second: That whether others do this or not, I will."

By age seven he had had a profound encounter with God, and at twelve he wrote about revival like a seasoned saint. Also at twelve he wrote his famous essay on the spider, which became a pioneer work in the history of American natural science.

But religion was his first love. Even as a child he would take his chums to a quiet place in the woods for prayer. Years after, as leader of the Great Awakening, he saw very young children do similar things. His own childhood experience provided the background for understanding such unusual events.

At seventeen Jonathan Edwards earned a B.A. from Yale, having entered at age thirteen. At nineteen he received his master's degree for academic work in preparation for the ministry. To this day may be seen an appropriate plaque in the outdoor corridors of Yale Divinity School to the honor of one of its most distinguished graduates, Jonathan Edwards.

Subsequent to his graduation he taught, and at age twenty-four was ordained and made associate minister with his maternal grandfather, Solomon Stoddard, at the Northampton, Massachusetts Congregational Church. Two years later, in 1729, his grandfather passed away and Jonathan became the full-time minister. The bulk of Edwards's writing was done during his twenty-three years at Northampton.

His remarkable wife, Sarah Pierrepont, was such a good domestic manager that he was at liberty to spend twelve or even thirteen hours a day in study, in addition to his pastoral duties.

Revival came in 1734, four years before Wesley's Aldersgate experience. In a six-month period, three hundred were converted in a town of only two hundred families. Over the years the revival spirit came and went, but when it was not in evidence, seed was being sown. When it was in evidence, harvest was taking place.

Toward the end of his ministry in Northampton, however, Edwards incurred the wrath of his people by what they considered an overly strict spiritual discipline. He refused to allow the unconverted and unrepentant to take Holy Communion, with the result that he was expelled from the church.

He left the pastorate to work in a mission for Indians in Stockbridge, Massachusetts (1751-1757). While there he wrote what some consider to be his most famous work, *The Freedom of the Will*, and a work on original sin.

Jonathan Edwards's final professional appointment was the presidency of the College of New Jersey (later Princeton University), but he was there only a month. He submitted to a smallpox inoculation. The vaccine was still in its experimental stages, and he contracted the disease and died.

But what a noble impact he had made, though he died in his fifties! Some have said his was the finest mind of colonial

America. John Greenleaf Whittier praised him in a poem which said that Edwards's conception of himself was minute while his love of others was gigantic. John Wesley thought enough of Edwards's *A Treatise Concerning Religious Affections* to make an abridgement of it (published after Wesley's death). One has observed that, "The American Tract Society must have distributed approximately one million copies of Edwards' various writings before it ceased to list them among its publications in 1829."

The circulation of his writings, however, by no means stopped with 1829. They are still very much known. Yale has recently issued his works, Ralph Turnbull has produced a well-circulated volume on his preaching, and hitherto unpublished writings have come to light only recently.

At about twenty, Edwards recorded in his journal that he had come alive to the knowledge of God as sovereign. His moment of spiritual illumination came when he read 1 Timothy 1:17: "Now unto the King eternal, immortal, invisible, the only wise God, be honour, and glory forever and ever. Amen." With this backdrop, he announced in later years that it was God Himself who brings revival. Whenever it comes, God always fulfills that Scripture, Isaiah 2:17, "And the loftiness of man shall be bowed down, and the haughtiness of men shall be made low: and the LORD alone shall be exalted in that day." He said the same about individual conversion. Only the sovereign God can convert a man. Conversion is the magnificent work of God's power which immediately changes the heart and fills the dead soul with life. Edwards expressed his ideas on conversion in his book, *A Faithful Narrative of the Surprising Work of God,* the very title of which reflects his attitude toward God's sovereignty.

Some of Edwards's sermons were over two hours long, which was not so uncommon in a day and age more leisurely than ours. Nonetheless, it is probably true that his delivery was dull at times. His voice was weak and not very commanding. He lacked many pulpit graces. He read his manuscripts; and one author, observing Edwards's nearsightedness, pictures him as clutching his papers in one hand, holding a candle in the other, and staring down at his words as he read. If this is an accurate picture, probably the only bodily action in his delivery came from turning the pages and slight turns of the head. Add to all this the fact that he was reportedly not a very imposing person, and one wonders how such a man could make so great an impact.

A number of reasons have been ventured for Edwards's renown: his clear logic, his deep devotion, his spiritual insight, his tenderness, and his piercing eye. (The superstitious townspeople accused him of "looking off" the rope in the steeple so that the bell fell and crashed into the church.)

Edwards himself gives part of the reason for his success when he cries out against "nice" preachers who play with speculations about divine knowledge and never give the people what they really need. He pointed out that people don't need to have their heads stored with knowledge as much as they need to have their hearts touched by God.

Edwards may not have raised his voice, he may not have had wide and noticeable gestures, but he spoke with a passion that communicated godly concern, and his people responded.

There is still another reason for Edwards's remarkable communicative success: he never uttered a single thing without thinking it through, without having clear and logical reasons, and without finding support in the Scripture. Actually, he was always in the business of thinking through his subject matter. Even on walks and while riding horseback through the woods, he would jot down items and pin them to his coat. When he returned to the parsonage, he wrote out the fuller explanation of the bits noted on the scraps. Sometimes, it is said, nearly the whole of his coat front would be covered with bits and pieces of paper.

As to the scriptural documentation, he was utterly biblical, and when he preached, his text sounded again and again through the sermon, like the knocking theme of a Beethoven symphony. This scriptural background to what he said gave authority and provided conviction.

There can be no doubt that Edwards was a spiritual and intellectual pulpit giant. The great intellect God gave him was used in His service. For this we can be profoundly grateful, and our prayer is that God will raise up more of his stature.

* * *

Attention is called especially to Ralph G. Turnbull, *Jonathan Edwards the Preacher* (Grand Rapids: Baker, 1958), and to J. C. Wolf, editor, *Jonathan Edwards on Evangelism* (Grand Rapids: Eerdmans, 1958).

CHARLES GRANDISON FINNEY

Revival Preacher

1792-1875

Charles G. Finney

CHARLES GRANDISON FINNEY

SEVERAL YEARS after the publication of his famous lectures on revival, Mr. Finney wrote a series of letters entitled *Revival Fire* "to all the friends, and especially all the ministers, of our Lord Jesus Christ." The letters, he believes, are a more mature evaluation of revivals of religion.

In them, he warns against superficial revivals. Superficiality is the product of easy preaching on man's sin. The depravity of the heart must be announced with vivid clarity. The manifestations of man's depravity must be exposed to the light of God's perfect law. For true revival to come, the sense of guilt must be sufficiently real so that sinners are actually convicted by the Holy Ghost, not just pricked by the spur of conscience. This is the preacher's task. Finney is at pains to underscore this point, following Wesley's pattern of preaching law before grace.

Superficial revival is also due to a dearth of divine influence. Finney has been accused of believing that man could, by an act of the will, almost regenerate himself. He admitted that he erred sometimes in not placing sufficient stress on the divine role. Many people have been moved by means used to create excitement. They have become hopeful without learning that the presence and the work of the Holy Spirit are necessary. Finney concludes that there is no authentic experience of God aside from the agency of the Spirit of God.

Charles Finney warned against unhealthy revival excitement. He stressed that true religion stems from intelligent obedience to God, not a response based upon emotion or fear. He believed that when feelings are supreme, the will tends to be incapacitated. The will, not the emotions, must rule; or else authentic religion does not take hold in the soul.

Does this mean that emotion has no role to play in revivals? No. Finney advocated just enough excitement to attract attention and guarantee attentiveness to the truth. But if excitement rules, people are deceived into believing they have something they haven't. Herein is the root of false hopes. Herein, too, is the cause of the intelligence taking a second place, which leads to mere enthusiasm and finally to fanaticism.

Mr. Finney warns that the leader in revival worship must walk a fine line when someone becomes too emotionally involved. To reprimand the individual harshly will shut off the flow of God's Spirit; to fan the emotional outburst into flames may result in the appearance of many coming to Chirst, but only the appearance. Finney warned that such events lead to evil.

Spurious revival preaching and leadership can be avoided by communicating scriptural truth, not mere philosophies of religion which puff up the mind. Finney believed that preaching metaphysical and philosophical speculations about religion encouraged the depraved, self-complacent, skeptical mind to believe that it comprehends all the great truths of God and His kingdom. They will substitute their wild fancies for true faith.

True Christians are detected by their meekness and humility, by the dominance of love in their lives, by the centrality of Christ, and by their love of the Scriptures. Certainly Finney would explain the elements of the gospel so far as one can. After all, he was a professor of religion at Oberlin College and then its president. But mere human speculation, couched in high flown terms, leads to error.

What will bring about revivals, declares Finney, is personal holiness, power in prayer, the authentic preaching of the Word, self-denial, and energetic effort. Revivals are absolutely necessary for the ongoing and growth of the church. Finney encouraged them to promote the church where members were dying faster than sinners were being converted to fill their places. Not only is the church promoted by revival, the whole of the national culture is influenced by it.

Finney knew the culture of his time. He had grown up in rural America, quite ignorant of the gospel, and knew from personal experience what God could do for a person. God transformed him as a young lawyer, made him thoroughly penitent and devout, and brought him to an intimate knowledge of the Scriptures. Finney knew that what had been done for him could be done for countless thousands. Great Britain and America were visibly moved by the revival he ushered in under God. As an evangelist, as a pastor, and as a college president, he saw changes in people. He saw transformed people go out to be used as instruments to change others around the world. He saw people changed through publications such as *Lectures on Revivals of Religion* and *Lectures to Professing Christians*. The fact is that the culture we breathe today, especially in our evangelical churches, is in part the product of Charles G. Finney's revivalism, for it was he who set the pattern.

His revival preaching is still our model in many respects. Simple, homey, always understandable, he preached sin and judgment with tears in his eyes and compassion in his heart.

If anything accounted for the dynamic effectiveness of Finney's preaching, it was prayer. The fabled Father Nash, who organized prayer groups for the evangelistic campaigns and prayed while Finney preached, symbolizes Finney's emphasis on prayer as the key to revival.

The six-foot evangelist, controlled and logical, leaves evangelicals a sobering and much needed directive. He warned against those who looked suspiciously or with disinterest on revival efforts, for revivals are the life and salvation of the church and the hope of the world. Rather than allow revivalism to die out, Finney encouraged ministers and Christians to increase revivals a hundredfold. Anyone who truly values his

own soul and the souls of other men should encourage revival as did Charles Grandison Finney.

* * *

Charles G. Finney's *Revival Fire,* reprinted in 1971 by Bethany
Fellowship of Minneapolis, is a primary source on his view of re-
vival preaching. V. Raymond Edman did a biography, *Finney
Lives On: The Man, His Revival Methods, and His Message*
(New York: Revell, 1951).

ARTHUR JOHN GOSSIP

Faithful Preacher

1873-1954

Arthur John Gossip

Rare photograph obtained from Dr. Gossip's son. Courtesy of Lowell O. Ryan.

ARTHUR JOHN GOSSIP

The Hero in Thy Soul, Being an Attempt to Face Life Gal-lantly, a book of sermons published in 1928, contains the best known sermon of Arthur John Gossip, "But When Life Tumbles In, What Then?" Originally, that sermon was delivered the Sunday after his wife passed away. He had sent her to the hospital for minor surgery, but she never came back. That he continued in faithful and productive ministry, never giving way to paralyzing discouragement, is only half the beauty of his life. The other half is that through suffering he became a better and more helpful servant of God.

A quick look at the sweep of his life reveals something of the extent of his contribution. He received his master's degree at Edinburgh, Scotland; pastored four churches—Liverpool, Forfar, Glasgow, Aberdeen; served as an army chaplain; and was professor of practical theology and Christian ethics at Trinity College, Glasgow.

When he began his ministry in Liverpool, he wrote a discouraged letter to Marcus Dods, complaining that his speech was poor and stammering, nothing like the eloquence of John Caird. Dods had no patience with his complaint. He sent a curt postcard announcing that there are those whom God is able to bring to Himself through John Caird and there are those He can draw with Arthur John Gossip. But he added that he was sure God knew His business well enough to appoint the right man to the right sphere of influence. Dods's final admonishment to Gossip was that he get on with *his* job in *his* own way.

He did indeed get on with it! In 1924, he published sermon studies entitled, *From the Edge of the Crowd;* in 1926, *The*

Galilean Accent; in 1944, *Experience Worketh Hope, Being Some Thoughts for a Troubled Day;* in 1947, *In the Secret Place of the Most High: Studies in Prayer.* Andrew W. Blackwood says his best work is found in the Warrack Lectures on preaching, *In Christ's Stead,* which was originally published in 1925.

Loaded with advice, his Warrack Lectures admonish the preacher to be himself. To emphasize that men do not need to be great to arrest attention, he quoted Anatole France: "If they have loved something, or hoped for something, and if they have left a part of themselves at the end of their pens, that is enough."

Symptoms of success are relatively unimportant. They may be few or many. The real sign of success is winning a soul. He quoted Père Didon: "Your influence over a soul is conditioned by the depth of your love for it; in order to save it and bring a divine influence to bear upon it, you must have a divine love for it." He warned that at times a preacher may become grumpy over "thin" pews. But he must take care that he does not suffer more from hurt pride than he does from hurt to the kingdom. Moreover, it is the consistent preaching of the gospel that is the most effective. Someone said that thirty years of preaching tend to look like thirty years of beating the air. The weekly drip, drip, drip wears in far deeper than we think. The knowledge of that fact helps provide staying power. Many a man has quit because he is not winning souls fast enough.

Gossip's treatment of the public reading of the Scriptures and the pastoral prayer are worth comment. He quoted a well-known preacher who said that of all the spiritual happenings of the ministry, most had come not through preaching but through the reading of the Bible. One needs to prepare himself with absorbed care for the public reading of God's Word. Scripture reading should not sound detestable—as though one were reading a stuffy speech. God's Word was meant to be read simply, reverently, and with feeling. Such a careful reading will inevitably touch some hearts.

As to the pastoral prayer, he quoted a working man in Glasgow who said that, without doubt, as far as he was concerned, the most important part of the service was intercessory prayer. He explained that often the common man is too weary to follow a discourse closely but can become involved in the ministry of prayer.

Gossip suggested that one way for the pastor to learn to pray publicly is to steep his mind in the classics of devotion written by great men of prayer. He can learn from their example and encouragement.

His view of preaching itself is summarized in this sentence: "Preaching resembles music in this respect, that for a real success three things are required—a theme worth hearing, a sufficient instrument, and a master whose deft touch can draw from both what his soul finds in them." The instruments are the living, throbbing hearts, minds, and wills of the listening men and women. The master with the deft stroke is the preacher, speaking out of a heart filled by God with the theme worth hearing.

From this he proceeds to discuss some resources for preaching. One is the life of the preacher. If he has experienced what he is talking about, then he has something he can communicate.

Another resource is reading. Someone said, "Not to read is to tempt God, though to do nothing but read is to neglect your office." Reading replenishes the mind; those who do not read repeat themselves and become boring. More, information is tucked away in the subconscious and may come forth at any time to serve us. Gossip tells of an item that came to his attention from reading thirty years previous which came to his rescue during the preparation of a sermon. He admits that forgetting what you read is a problem, and quotes Muhammad who complained that, study the Koran though he would, it "kept slipping away, like a camel whose leg was not tied."

Nature is another resource for preaching. Wordsworth's servant said to a visitor, pointing to the poet's library, "This is his library, but his study is outside."

Human nature, too, is a resource. Alexander Whyte said that the worst advice he ever got was when his session said he needn't bother about this business of going in and out of houses. He visited and had little district meetings. It delighted him to get next to his people. Pastoral calling, said A. J. Gossip, was to make people feel that Christ is with them in their homes. Getting next to people helps a minister by showing him that people want God. He illustrates this with the account of a crowd of gypsies following a man of God. They cried, "Give us God." He threw money to them. "We don't want your money," they shouted. "Give us God." Further, we learn that behind placid faces are people in desperate need—gallant, uncomplaining people who come to church to get strength for another week.

Our preaching must have about it that quiet assurance that our converts will do well. We must just expect that they will go on in the faith. Goethe teaches that whatever you want a man to be, you must assume he is. Gossip believed this was Christ's method. When he was a chaplain in World War I, the soldiers used to come to him just after entering the service and ask if he thought they would do all right. He always reassured them by telling them that they wore the uniform of a great battalion so people would assume their success. He used the same firm but quiet assumptive tactic in claiming that men who were born again through the preaching in the church would of course stay true. Such reassurance and confidence was more effective than fierce renunciations and flaming appeals.

Just as the attitudes behind the preaching of Dr. Gossip are instructive, so also are his ideas on sermon production in his

Warrack Lectures. First, Dr. Gossip says there is no making of the sermon without physical exercise. Whether it be golfing, walking, or whatever, one must have it. A. J. Gossip said the best advice he ever received from a doctor parishioner was on a Monday. He said, "A little liverish weren't you, yesterday? I thought I would look in and recommened some exercise." (Gossip had preached gloomily on Sunday.)

Second, choose your subject early in the week, then do not change it. Dr. Gossip told of the preacher who wasted energy by changing his subject Saturday night weekly, then staying up all night to write the new sermon. Have a rough outline down by Tuesday morning. Then shake it about like hay in the sun as you make your calls and do your pastoral work through the week.

Third, reduce your outline to writing. In his early ministry, Dr. Gossip took great pains writing out every word. When he got into the army, he had neither leisure nor place to do that. But the early discipline came to his rescue. He had learned how to put language together orally. When he left the chaplaincy, he did not need to return to writing.

Fourth, take infinite pains. Johnson once told Reynolds the secret of success: Every time he spoke, to great or small audiences, he took care to express himself well.

Finally, follow Schopenhauer's four guidelines for writers: (1) have something to say; (2) write carefully so that everyone knows you put importance on what you have to say; (3) use clear, simple language which shows that your ideas have been thought through thoroughly; (4) remember: the simpler the expression, the deeper the impression.

"You spoke as if you had come straight from the Presence," a stranger said to Whyte. "Perhaps I did," he answered shyly. "Given that," says Gossip, "the poorest stick of us will catch fire. Preach not doctrine, but Christ. Let them see that wonderful figure."

An American was sitting in one of Arthur Gossip's services

in a village church. As Gossip got up to preach, the visitor seemed to see Christ behind the preacher; and as Gossip progressed with his sermon, Christ became bigger and bigger until Gossip was not seen at all. Only Christ was there.

That was what Arthur John Gossip wanted more than anything.

*   *   *

One of the great books in the Warrack Lectures series is Arthur John Gossip's *In Christ's Stead,* first published in 1925, the year of the lectures, and now available in paperback (Grand Rapids: Baker, 1968).

His sermon "But When Life Tumbles In, What Then?" can be found in the American edition of *The Hero in Thy Soul* published by Scribners in New York in 1929.

BILLY GRAHAM
Authoritative Preacher
1918-

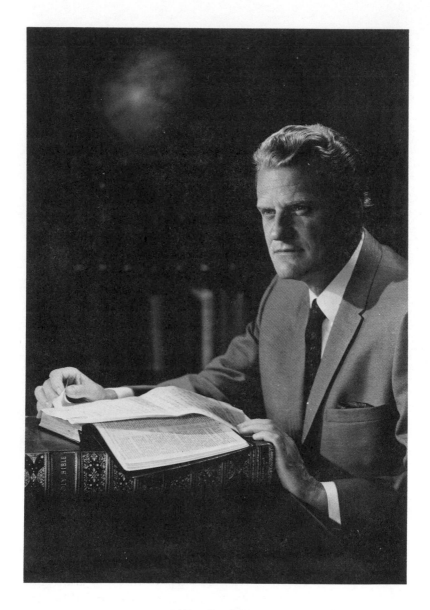

Billy Graham

BILLY GRAHAM

JUST BEFORE the 1949 crusade, Billy Graham had doubts about the Bible. He thought he saw apparent contradictions. "Some things I could not reconcile with my restricted concept of God."

When he stood to preach, he lacked authority. "Like hundreds of other young seminary students, I was waging the intellectual battle of my life. The outcome could certainly affect my future ministry."

The outcome of his struggle is well known: "In August of that year I had been invited to Forest Home, Presbyterian conference center high in the mountains outside Los Angeles. I remember walking down a trail, tramping into the woods, and almost wrestling with God. I dueled with my doubts, and my soul seemed to be caught in the crossfire. Finally, in desperation, I surrendered my will to the living God revealed in Scripture. I knelt before the open Bible and said 'Lord, many things in this Book I do not understand. But Thou hast said, "The just shall live by faith." All I have received from Thee, I have taken by faith. Here now, by faith, I accept the Bible as Thy Word. I take it all. I take it without reservations. Where there are things I cannot understand, I will reserve judgment until I receive more light. If this pleases Thee, give me authority as I proclaim Thy Word, and through that authority convict me of sin and turn sinners to the Saviour.' "

Within six weeks the Los Angeles Crusade was under way. During that campaign Billy discovered the secret that changed his ministry. "I stopped trying to prove that the Bible was true. I had settled in my own mind that it was, and this faith was conveyed to the audience. Over and over again I found

77

myself saying 'The Bible says.' " Billy felt as if he were the mouthpiece of the Spirit of God.

He discovered, too, that there was authority in that kind of preaching. With the authority came faith; and with faith, response. Hundreds responded, and the Los Angeles tent meeting scheduled to be three weeks lasted for eight.

The hunderds of thousands who attended were starved to hear from God Himself. "I felt as though I had a rapier in my hand and, through the power of the Bible, was slashing deeply into men's consciences, leading them to surrender to God."

The Bible became a flame in his hands, melting away unbelief, and moving men to decide for Christ.

Mr. Graham found further that "I did not have to rely upon cleverness, oratory, psychological manipulation of crowds, or apt illustrations or striking quotations from famous men. I began to rely more and more upon Scripture itself, and God blessed."

Billy added, "Belief exhilarates the human spirit; doubt depresses. Nothing is gained psychologically or spiritually by casting aspersions on the Bible. A generation that occupied itself with criticism of the Scriptures all too soon found itself questioning divine revelation."

Further, he is convinced, from experience of preaching around the world, that "the average American is vulnerable to the Christian message if it is seasoned with authority and proclaimed as verily from God through His Word."

Thus, his admonition to preachers is "Give a new centrality to the Bible in your own preaching. . . . The fire in your heart and on your lips can kindle a sacred flame in some cold hearts and win them to Christ. . . . Preach the Scriptures with authority! You will witness a climactic change in your ministry!"

With the authoritative rapier in his hand, Graham saw well-known figures from Southern California come to Christ.

Jim Vaus, today in significant Christian work in New York; Stuart Hamblen, author of "It Is No Secret What God Can Do"; Louis Zamperini, track star; and many others came to Christ. The conversion of the famous people caught the attention of William Randolph Hearst, who made the now famous command: "Puff Graham." The Los Angeles *Examiner* and Hearst papers across the nation told the story. The Graham movement was launched.

Before that, William Franklin Graham was little known. True, he had been a successful pastor in Wheaton, active in Youth for Christ, and an evangelist. But since 1949 he has been the leading evangelist of the world. He has, in fact, addressed more than fifty million people in over two hundred crusades and one-night stands. More, he has carried on a vast radio program; employed his pen in a vigorous book, pamphlet, and tract enterprise; and appeared on secular, as well as religious TV.

Southern Baptist Theological Seminary in Louisville has a Billy Graham Room. In it are key documents symbolizing the progress of the movement. What new items will that room house in the future? What fresh approaches will the Graham Association take? The following developments would lead one to think along several lines.

Billy Graham Associate Evangelist Leighton Ford read a position paper at the US Congress on Evangelism that would suggest a greater effort to reach intellectuals. The tone and character of the paper have authentic appeal to alert young minds. Ford enjoys a growing audience, and other evangelists on the Graham roster have intellectual gifts which could be used with fine effectiveness in the university communities.

Dr. Graham's Swiss son-in-law, living near the beautiful lakeside city of Montreux, could symbolize a whole new ministry with businessmen on an international level. He himself is an aggressive young businessman and has an impressive influence.

Women will have an even wider ministry in the future. During the Anaheim Crusade, Mrs. Graham spoke to the largest group of her career at the biggest banquet ever set west of the Mississippi—eleven hundred strong.

The future of the Billy Graham Evangelistic Association will be interesting to watch in the growth of *Decision* magazine, the book ministry, extended worldwide outreach, and the emergence of previously unthought of methods of gospel propagation.

*   *   *

The quotations in this chapter are taken from Billy Graham's article, "Biblical Authority and Evangelism," *Christianity Today,* Oct. 15, 1956, pp. 5-7, 17. Used by permission.

Decision magazine carries a regular sermon by Mr. Graham. Those coupled with his sermons in delivery over TV are good resources for analyzing Graham's approach to preaching.

MARTIN LUTHER
Indefatigable Preacher

1483-1546

Martin Luther

From a bronze statue in Eisleben, by Siemering, 1883, reprinted from *Martin Luther, the Man and His Work* by Arthur C. McGiffert (New York: Century, 1917), facing page 13.

MARTIN LUTHER

How DIFFERENT were the two reformers Luther and Melancthon. The latter was quiet, refined, every inch the scholar. Luther was fiery, roughhewn. He was always out on the firing line—in the classroom, in debate, in heated discussion, and especially in the preaching situation.

No one knows how many times he stood to preach. Luther's extant sermons are estimated at twenty-three hundred. The new Concordia edition of Luther's works includes several volumes of sermons—three volumes on John 1-16 alone.

An impassioned and empowered St. Paul of sixteenth century Germany, he preached anywhere he could and every time he got a chance. He preached to the monks in his Augustinian monastery; preached three days before he died, and even wrote sermons for others to preach.

Commissioned to preach in Wittenberg City Church, he preached three times on Sunday: in the morning, at five or six P.M. (in series on a book of the Bible), and then at eight or nine P.M. He preached daily: Monday and Tuesday he did catechetical sermons (some became the basis for his smaller and larger catechisms); the rest of the week he devoted to various books of the New Testament. How consistent this Wittenberg schedule was throughout his years there (1514-1522) we do not know; what is clear is his tirelessness in preaching and the sense of urgency that possessed him. Luther even preached at his home when he was too ill to ascend a pulpit, especially 1532-34.

Martin Luther's sermons were not so much the product of the writing table as they were the result of a burning soul which had to express itself. He preached some sermons without texts. Ideas and words rushed out spontaneously, almost compulsively.

Luther did not have time to set down in writing his ideas about preaching; that is, not in anything like full manuscript form. His contemporaries, Melanchthon and Erasmus, did produce books on public rhetoric. Nonetheless, we can glean from Luther's writings comments here and there which reveal his concept of the preacher and his task.

He believed the congregation ought never to come together without the preaching or expounding of the Word and prayers. As a boy, Luther had never heard the Bible explained; thus, he was driven to do expository preaching.

To Luther, the highest eloquence was to speak simply, like Jesus. When he spoke, he did not concentrate so much on the doctors and teachers in attendance as on the young people, children and servants.

Not only did Luther believe in simplicity, but he stressed that preaching should be slow and calm without shouting and histrionics.

The preacher must be possessed of prophetic courage. He must be willing to venture everything to preach the Word. At times he may suffer ridicule, but he must be just as fearless as Luther was.

While Luther had some suggestions as to method, he himself refused to be poured into any mold. Thus writers refer to his style as heroic. His speech was characterized by strength and manliness. He spoke from his soul. One who heard him preach described his style as "spontaneous impetuosity."

Luther compared preachers who do not stick to their subjects to servant girls who stop to talk to everyone on their way to the market. He stressed that one must have a theme and continue with it without rambling.

Above all he asserted that a sermon must not be long. Some of his own sermons were ten minutes, others were longer. Nevertheless, he pressed his point: Know when to stop!

With delightful humor, Martin Luther told of the preacher who addressed an audience of elderly women in a hospital on the subject of marriage! His point: the sermon should be adapted to the situation.

Finally, preparation must be done as carefully as a mother would prepare food for her baby.

There can be no doubt that Luther sometimes broke his own homiletical rules, but he communicated the deep convictions of his burning soul, and thousands came to hear him. Once, nearly a whole village left their harvesting and came to the church to hear him. Another time, he spoke from a city hall window to a crowd of twenty-five thousand in the marketplace below.

But it was not always that way. He had his ordinary routine days; and when he first mounted the pulpit, back at the outset of his preaching ministry, he confessed that he trembled. He argued with Staupitz as to whether his vocation was really preaching because it caused him such agony that he thought he would die. The doctor emphasized the great importance of the Lord's service.

Luther said yes to the divine summons. In so doing he pioneered in restoring preaching to its central place in the service of worship. Moreover, his sermons were published as tracts; and such a flow of sermons and other materials came from his lips and pen that Gordon Rupp, the British authority on Luther, calls him the Shakespeare of Germany.

The heart of Luther's motivation is seen in his beautiful words: "When you are about to preach, speak with God, 'Dear Lord God, I will preach to Thy honor and speak of Thee.' "

*   *   *

Concordia Publishing, St. Louis, Missouri, has brought out a multivolumed edition of *Luther's Works,* edited by J. Pelikan. The set includes his sermons, giving firsthand exposure to his recorded preaching.

A great biography of our day is Roland Bainton's, *Here I Stand* (New York: Abingdon, 1950).

CLARENCE EDWARD MACARTNEY

Careful Preacher

1879-1957

Clarence E. Macartney
Courtesy of the Presbyterian Church, Pittsburgh.

CLARENCE EDWARD MACARTNEY

THERE WAS GOOD REASON for Clarence Macartney to make preaching his life. His mother was born in Scotland, the land of great preachers; his father had gone to Glasgow as a youth to study theology and became an impressive preacher. Scottish Presbyterianism, with its noble emphasis on the proclamation of the Word, pervaded his life.

Dr. Macartney made Biblical preaching his life. Two days before his death, he said these now well-known words to his brother, Robertson, who was on his way to preach in a nearby church, "Put all the Bible you can into it."

There you have it! The statement was no mere theory. Dr. Macartney preached right from the Bible throughout his career in three major pastorates: Paterson, New Jersey (1905), Philadelphia (1914), and Pittsburgh (1927-53). The Bible was his textbook. He lived by the Bible, believed its truths, and proclaimed them with evident conviction. Frequently he spoke on the great charcters of the Bible. It was said that there was "hardly a [biblical] scene which he did not illuminate with his rare powers of description."

Dr. Macartney was a life-long student of communication and homiletics. As a university student, he was deeply involved in debating societies and thought of becoming a lawyer. Upon graduation he was, for a time, on the staff of a newspaper and actually considered a career in journalism. Newspaper reporting taught him clear communication. He also learned that human life is always an interesting drama.

He loved to write and speak, to study speeches and speakers, seeming never to tire of studying communication and, most particularly, communicators themselves.

It was, of course, to homiletics that he gave his greatest en-

89

ergies. He mastered pulpit communication techniques which found expression in serial, doctrinal, and dialogue sermons. He would, for example, play the parts of both the believer and the doubter. Doctrinal sermons are particularly difficult to rescue from the clutches of dullness, but Dr. Macartney was convinced that nothing could be as interesting and vital to the majority of people as the great doctrines of the Christian faith.

His famous sermon, "Come Before Winter," was first preached October 10, 1915; and every subsequent autumn he repeated it. Hundreds were greatly benefited, and the gripping evangelistic conclusion must have brought many to Jesus Christ. It is a superb example of evangelical communication.

Altogether, Dr. Macartney became one of America's finest communicators, a fact evidenced not only by his employment as a lecturer in homiletics at Princeton Seminary, but more eloquently by the hundreds who flocked to hear him week after week.

I once asked a Scottish preacher friend of Dr. Macartney's why he was such a good communicator. "Ah," he replied with a gleam in his eye, "preaching was his life. He lived to preach."

Another asset of Dr. Macartney's ministry was his development of extrabiblical sources. A fundamental principle of his life was that vacations must improve his mind and increase his fund of information. Thus he made frequent trips at home and abroad.

He must have followed the same principle in hobbies, because his interests in Lincoln and the Civil War, in national and international history, provided a vast store of information. Interestingly enough, he produced several volumes on Lincoln and the Civil War: *Lincoln and His Generals, Highways and By-Ways of the Civil War,* and others. On numerous occasions he met with Carl Sandburg to talk about Mr. Lincoln.

Still another resource grew out of his love of English literature. He was interested in Dean Swift and once presented a lecture on his life and works. On one of his trips abroad, he visited the tomb of Charles Wolfe, the Irish poet he so greatly admired.

Dr. Macartney lived close to his people. *The Making of a Minister,* his autobiography, makes it abundantly clear that he loved his people and preached to their needs. He writes about the beautiful affections of the ordinary people and describes the human heart in sensitive language. It was his habit to visit in homes and hospitals three or four afternoons a week.

He was remarkably creative in developing techniques to get next to people. He held summer services in the evening on the church lawn, conducted men's meetings on Tuesdays at noon, began services for medical students, and developed many more ideas for outreach. The result was a preaching ministry related to the lives of the people.

Dr. Macartney gave himself to the minister's task. He produced forty-seven books, many of them sermons, which reflect the hard work of his lifetime. He tended to business, never allowing time to slip through his fingers like sand at the seashore.

He preached without notes. He mastered his materials and then delivered them without recourse to notes of any kind. This he did at least five times a week, for that was the number of sermons and speaking engagements he regularly had in Pittsburgh. Sometimes there were more than that!

The security of thorough preparation was the secret of his free and easy speech. He didn't have to overpower people when he spoke. He always held the attention of his audience.

To add to his charm as a speaker, he was stately and held himself erect. A friend said that just to see him standing commanded attention.

Toward the close of his life, Dr. Macartney raised the common question, "If I had my life to live over, what would I change?" His answer reflects his insight and humility. He decided that he would devote more time to prayer, take more time for meditation, and study the Bible even more, even though his preaching had been based entirely on the Bible. He would take more time off to avoid the risk of ill health, for he confessed that he worked too many long hours. He had had no serious illness until late in his life; but he thought that, if he had been ill earlier, he might have learned to take better care of himself and have gained greater understanding and sympathy for others in their suffering.

But there was a basic pattern of ministry he would not change which he had tested and proved over a lifetime of service. That pattern consisted of preaching the truths of the Bible; faithfulness in pastoral visitation; continuous reading, study, and writing; travel; serial preaching; emphasis on evening services; and preaching without notes. This pattern reflects the care that Dr. Macartney took in his ministry and bears witness that preaching was his life.

* * *

Clarence E. Macartney's autobiography, *The Making of a Minister,* edited with an introduction by J. Clyde Henry and including a foreword by Frank E. Gaebelein, was published in 1961 by the Channel Press of Great Neck, New York.

PETER MARSHALL
Dynamic Preacher
1902-1949

Peter Marshall
Courtesy of Mrs. Peter (Catherine) Marshall.

PETER MARSHALL

CATHERINE MARSHALL was a most gracious and delightful person on that mild summer's day in Edinburgh in 1951. She had come to Scotland to do last minute research on her soon-to-be-published *A Man Called Peter*. Scurrying around seeing this person and that, visiting here and there, her time had been fully occupied; but now she could take an hour or two to relax with two couples from the university and enjoy a good cup of Scottish tea.

Perfectly free to talk about her late husband in the most natural manner, she made him seem almost alive again. His nobility of character and the fact that he had a heart after God came through, and one began to get a glimpse of why he had become one of the most dynamic evangelical preachers of our century.

Even though it has been twenty years since that afternoon cup of tea, let me share my impression of Catherine Marshall's informal and lively conversation about her husband. These impressions are no doubt colored by subsequent reading and exposure of one kind and another.

First, I was impressed by Dr. Marshall's passion for drawing his people closer to God. The very intensity of his preaching and public prayer communicated his passion. There was a sincerity, an earnestness, an emotional involvement that said, "I must communicate God."

Then, Peter Marshall had a flare for illuminating language that caught attention—not to be clever, but to draw his listeners to contemplate God. If somehow he could get their attention, even for a few moments, perhaps then they would focus on Him and in that very moment of focus, He might come and change them.

95

This is why he spoke of "the bifocals of faith," "the tribunal of my own conscience," "the tap on the shoulder." This is the rationale behind such lively language as "jealousy swallowed up in brotherly love," "the problem of lust masquerading as love," being delivered from "the tyranny of trifles." Everywhere one looks in Peter Marshall's printed sermons and prayers, vivid and vigorous language appears. He wanted to draw people to God.

Again, Peter Marshall was genuinely human. He had a touch that said, "I'm on your side. If I can help you, I want to try."

It was his own life of struggle that gave him this gift of rapport with people. As a young man in Scotland, he had worked desperately hard, almost to the point of impairing his health. He had come finally to America where he gave himself completely to his seminary training and preparation. He married an attractive Southern girl and went into pastoral work. But his difficulties did not end. His lovely wife contracted tuberculosis, and Peter struggled to keep his house in order, to find time to be a father to his small son, and to pastor his people. Finally he saw Catherine healed, but in time he himself became ill with a heart ailment.

His own suffering was the background out of which he spoke to people, and somehow the pathos of his life communicated that he knew very well the troubles, spoken or unspoken, that his parishoners were going through.

He didn't try to dodge the hard things in life; he faced them constructively. His father died when he was young, and he had to "fetch" for himself. For one period he worked in a steel mill for nine hours a day and went to school at night. He was compelled to drop out of school because of the limitations of time, money, and energy.

All this geared him to a vigorous acceptance of life. He learned to take it in stride and constantly strove to abolish the wrong and build up the right.

Then, his moral stature was strong and obvious to all who came into contact with him. It was not only his popularity as an evangelical preacher or his flare for attention-getting language that made the Senate invite him to be their chaplain. It was also that Washington knew what he stood for, and to have him stand regularly before the Senate was in itself a message of righteousness.

When he talked to young people, he held high the banner of purity and Christlikeness. Because he could speak the language of the young, they accepted his messages; and no one knows the tremendous influence he had on scores of them.

The final impression I came away with that day was Dr. Marshall's love for his countries. He could never forget his native Scotland with its heather, its music, and its kilts. Nor could he have been more appreciative of the United States. Scotland had given him a heritage that spelled out strong character, godly preaching, and undivided loyalites. America had given him opportunity, and the very fact that he could come here and succeed under God never ceased to grip him. The day that he was made a naturalized citizen was a proud day for him; the day he was invited to become chaplain of the United States Senate was as exciting a day as he had ever known. Peter Marshall linked the deep appreciation for his heritage with patriotic zeal for his adopted country.

To summarize, Dr. Peter Marshall had a desire to see his people brought to God, a flare for creative language, a spirit that would not give in, a zeal for righteousness, and a deep sense of loyalty to God and country. It is no surprise that his name and influence live on!

* * *

Catherine Marshall gave us *A Man Called Peter: The Story of Peter Marshall* (New York: McGraw-Hill, 1951) .

Dr. Marshall's sermon manuscript style is observable in the sermon book, *Mr. Jones, Meet the Master* (Old Tappan, N.J.: Revell, 1949) .

FREDERICK BROTHERTON MEYER

Enterprising Preacher

1847-1929

Frederick Brotherton Meyer

After the portrait by John Collier, reprinted from *F. B. Meyer, A Biography* by W. Y. Fullerton (Marshall, Morgan & Scott, n.d.), frontispiece.

FREDERICK BROTHERTON MEYER

THE MOST OUTSTANDING THING that may be said of F. B. Meyer is that he was always conscious of the presence of God. Canon Earp described him as a man of God who did not try to impress but presented his simple message sincerely, revealing his own soul. That transparency enabled him to make immediate contact with his people in or out of the pulpit.

Meyer himself explained his consciousness of God's presence in this way: "Deep fellowship with Christ is impossible unless you set yourself to its cultivation. Friendship cannot be made by glimpses."

He had a deep conviction that fresh springs would well up continually in one's religious life if one is close to the Lord. Those springs bubbled joyously for sixty-six years of gospel ministry. His amazingly productive ministry took a variety of shapes.

One of the aspects of Meyer's frutiful ministry was writing. Although he is chiefly remembered for his Bible biographies, he also wrote travelogues, his autobiography, twelve volumes on Christian living, Bible expositions, volumes of sermons, essays, and booklets to enclose in letters. In all, he wrote thirty pamphlets and produced seventy volumes, many of which were translated into foreign languages. By 1929, one firm alone had circulated over 2.5 million volumes of Meyer's work. He also edited two magazines, *Worship and Work* and *Christian Treasury*. Throughout all his works is an explanation of and exhortation to the vigorous life in the Spirit.

Then, F. B. Meyer is remembered for his preaching. He liked open-air speaking most of all. During his Leicester days, he preached on the street three times a week. Melbourne

Hall was built there to hold twelve hundred people, and often it was filled.

In London, the Sunday evening congregation began at about a hundred. In a few years, the attendance had risen to two thousand or more. At Christ Church, London, the attendance doubled in his four years of ministry.

F. B. Meyer served as an assistant to Dr. C. M. Birrell at Pembroke Chapel, Liverpool, in his early days. Dr. Birrell inspired him to practice expository preaching. He made it his lifelong habit.

When he began preaching, Meyer was very meticulous. He would write, revise, and rewrite; and sometimes he spent hours preparing the introduction alone. In later years his preparation became more natural, but it may be ventured that his later fluency and power in discourse were due, at least in part, to the early years of discipline.

James McGraw, in *Great Evangelical Preachers of Yesterday,* gives us Meyer's later method of sermon preparation. First, he selected the text early in the week. The rest of the week he spent mulling it over in his mind. Second, he recorded his thoughts on paper. Then he read relevant materials. In due course, the thrust of the message emerged.

Sometimes, however, the central thought did not appear until one or two hours before delivery; but he was not concerned because he relied on his mind to organize the message automatically.

The missionary impact of Dr. F. B. Meyer's life was formidable. He visited Europe, Jamaica, the USA, Canada, the Near East, China, India, South Africa, and Australia in the days before air travel! In the States he spoke repeatedly for D. L. Moody, especially at the famous Northfield Conferences.

He served as acting director and general secretary of the Regions Beyond Missionary Union. He was also a supporter of the London Missionary Society and the China Inland Mission, whose founder, James Hudson Taylor, was his personal friend.

Meyer's parishioners were expected to be home missionaries too. He even told his people not to hear him twice on Sunday if they could reach someone for Christ during the worship service.

Today, F. B. Meyer is also remembered as a great social reformer who aimed to improve society through the reformation of individuals. He was driven in his task by a tireless compassion.

He became involved in the formation of the Purity, Rescue, and Temperance Organization of the Central South London Free Church Council, which closed over eleven hundred houses of prostitution and rescued hundreds of women. Continuing in his desire to help others, he helped establish the Homeless Children's Aid and Adoption Society, the F. B. Meyer Children's Home, and, the Society for Befriending the Unmarried Mother and Child. Through these three agencies, over two thousand children were helped and about one thousand were adopted.

Meyer's Spirit-given compassion led him to prison in Leicester, not as a convict but as a man interested in helping those about to be released to make plans for their return to society. Then, when a man was released, Meyer took him to a nearby restaurant rather than allow him to resort to the nearest tavern. His interest in delinquency spurred the development of Providence House for boys who were potential criminals.

In London, he spent his Sunday afternoons in the slum district preaching Christ to the men there. As many as eight hundred men gathered to hear him, and many were converted.

Other works for men in which he served were men's brotherhoods, the YMCA, and a coffee shop and clubhouse (of which he was the proprietor) where men could gather for games and talk.

Someone has said that F. B. Meyer was at his best with children, so naturally, he was interested in Sunday schools. In Leicester, he rented three halls and built a Sunday school of twenty-five hundred children. In London, he supervised eight Sunday schools with a total enrollment of four thousand. In May of 1907, he was elected president of the World's Sunday School Association.

His passion to help people is epitomized in the words of W. Y. Fullerton in *F. B. Meyer, a Biography:* "Mr. Meyer's views of religion are those of a man who has toiled and suffered, not so much for himself as for others, which is mainly where his strength comes in." It is no wonder that many hundreds attended the funeral services of this good man.

* * *

Now out of print, the eager student of preaching should scour the used-book stores and catalogs for W. Y. Fullerton's *F. B. Meyer, a Biography* (London: Marshall, Morgan & Scott, n.d.).

James McGraw's *Great Evangelical Preachers of Yesterday* (New York: Abingdon, 1961) includes a chapter on Meyer.

DWIGHT LYMAN MOODY
Surrendered Preacher
1837-1899

Dwight L. Moody

DWIGHT LYMAN MOODY

"I CAN TRULY SAY, and in saying it I magnify the infinite grace of God as bestowed upon him, that I have seen few persons whose minds were spiritually darker than was his when he came into my Sunday school class; and I think the committee of the Mount Vernon Church seldom met an applicant for membership more unlikely ever to become a Christian of clear and decided views of gospel truth, still less to fill any extended sphere of public usefulness." So wrote Edward Kimball, the man who won young Dwight Moody to Christ.

It all came about in an interesting way. Moody had left Northfield, Massachusetts, the town of his birth, in a fit of rebellion against his farm job. He decided to sell shoes for a relative who owned his own store in the big city of Boston. In the city, he attended Mount Vernon Congregational Church, and Edward Kimball was his Sunday school teacher. That man, imbued with a passion to win every one of his Sunday school boys to Christ, went to see Moody one day. In the back of the store he talked with him straightforwardly about salvation. The two knelt among the shoe boxes. There, the husky youth, Dwight Moody, wept tears of repentance. His was no passing experience; he had truly met God.

In time, Dwight moved to Chicago where he continued in the shoe business. He became so good at his trade that a saying grew up in the store, "Give the tough customers to Moody." Had Moody not become an evangelist, he would likely have gone to the top in business. Actually, the salesman in him is easily seen in a sermon such as "What Think Ye of Christ?" His calculated plan to secure a decision for Christ was like closing a sale.

When Moody moved from Boston to Chicago, he joined

107

the Plymouth Congregational Church. So enthusiastic was he for the spread of the gospel that he had experienced that he rented four pews and filled them right away with men and boys. He seemed cut out to be an evangelist from his early days as a Christian. Restless to do more, he joined the Mission Band of First Methodist Church and went with youthful eagerness to saloons, hotels, and cheap lodging houses distributing tracts. Next, he found a little Sunday school one block from where Moody Bible Institute is today. When he asked to teach a class, he was told that he could teach any new people he brought in. The next Sunday saw eighteen barefooted, dirty-faced urchins in his class! Soon, due to his proddings, the Sunday school was filled to overflowing.

A piece of driftwood on the shores of Lake Michigan was the location for the beginnings of Moody Memorial Church. That part of his life began in the summer of 1858, when he started with a small class. By September there were too many for the log, so he rented a saloon. When that was outgrown, he moved to a larger hall, but kept the saloon for prayer meetings. Within a year there were six hundred people to divide into eighty classes! Then the attendance jumped to a thousand, and on Sundays there were fifteen hundred. All this time Dwight Moody was still selling shoes, but after 1860 he devoted himself entirely to religious work.

Mr. Moody had little formal education. He never mastered grammar, spelling, or pronunciation. When he was nervous, he stammered; but determination and the grace of God saw him overcome that hurdle. To make matters worse, his mother was a Unitarian and could not understand her son's desire to become a preacher.

In spite of these handicaps he became a world-famous evangelist. Why? In a meeting Moody had heard someone say, "It remains to be seen what God can do if He can find a man who will completely surrender to Him!" Moody left the meeting determined to be that man.

See what this surrendered man, under God, accomplished. He established a school for girls at Northfield, Mt. Hermon Academy for boys, a training school for religious workers, a Bible Conference, and the Moody Bible Institute in Chicago, which has a current enrollment of more than a thousand full-time students.

The Encyclopedia Americana says that Moody's marked executive ability caused men of wealth to contribute generously to his institutions. In both Chicago and Northfield, he established publishing outlets; and his brother-in-law, Fleming H. Revell, began the well-known publishing house to promote the Moody cause. In addition, the Moody-Sankey *Sacred Songs and Solos* sold some ten million copies, yielding a royalty of one million dollars, every cent of which was given for philanthropic purposes.

In 1870, Ira D. Sankey joined Moody. The two did a preaching tour of England and Scotland and witnessed there a religious awakening unparalleled since the days of Wesley. On their return to the States, large meetings were held in New York, Brooklyn, and Philadelphia. Subsequently Moody preached in every major city of the United States, and it is estimated that he addressed over fifty million people. They came to hear a man paint word pictures in warm and homely language and to hear Sankey play and sing. Fun and humor were not wanting in the meetings, but the preaching of the Word of God was supreme, for Moody discovered early in his evangelistic work that the secret of Spirit-filled preaching that led men to Jesus Christ was the exposition of the Bible.

One more thing—Moody saw the value of winning men. He, perhaps more than any other, was responsible for establishing the YMCA in America, an institution which in those days specialized in Bible study, personal evangelism, Bible conferences, and street preaching. He set up a program for systematic tract distribution and preaching to men in prisons. He worked at Camp Douglas, just about where the University of Chicago is today, during the Civil War. And so it went; he was a man's man, and it was in him to win men.

That, in a brief sketch, is the story of a surrendered man. Perhaps it is not so strange that a man of Henry Drummond's stature should call Dwight Lyman Moody "the biggest human I ever met."

*   *   *

A number of Moody biographies are available, including John Pollock's *Moody: A Biographical Portrait* (Grand Rapids: Zondervan, 1963) and Faith Coxe Bailey's *D. L. Moody* (Chicago: Moody, 1959), a paperback.

The Best of D. L. Moody, compiled by Wilbur M. Smith (Chicago: Moody, 1971), contains sixteen of Moody's greatest sermons.

G. CAMPBELL MORGAN
Biblical Preacher
1863-1945

George Campbell Morgan
Courtesy of Revell Publishing Company.

G. CAMPBELL MORGAN

GEORGE CAMPBELL MORGAN, a powerful and unique Bible preacher, was born and educated in England. Always he retained that marvelous characteristic of English public speakers—the power of vivid and incisive communication. His written work is characterized by that same quality.

G. Campbell Morgan's life was an active one. Ordained to the gospel ministry in 1889, he pastored in both England and America, was a popular Northfield Conference extension speaker, engaged in YMCA work in London, and traveled widely, preaching and lecturing.

His writing alone staggers the imagination. Sixty books and eleven pamphlets, plus *The Analyzed Bible,* came from his pen. The latter is the Revised Version of the Bible put out by Oxford University Press, with an analysis and the message of each book of the Holy Scriptures. His books circulated widely and are reported to have numbered over a million copies.

Thousands came to hear him preach and teach the Scriptures. The fact is that the one aim of his remarkable life was to make the Bible clear, and he accomplished that goal to a degree as remarkable as his life.

G. Campbell Morgan was an incisive student. Herein is the key to the charm and drawing power of the man. He was ever a student, always learning, constantly coming up with fresh and engaging material. One simply cannot read him, just as no one could hear him, without becoming a richer person. He was constantly delving deeper and deeper into the Greek and English texts of the Scriptures.

But the principle that guided all this study was fundamental to his discoveries and the exciting observations he shared.

113

That principle he called the "contextual principle" of Bible interpretation. By it he simply meant that a passage must always be viewed in its contexts, immediate and larger. Scripture interprets Scripture. An isolated text is not really isolated: it is part of a complete literary unit, and that unit is in turn part of a larger unit. Eventually the text must be viewed as part of the whole of Scripture.

The contextual principle protected Dr. Morgan from silly interpretations, inevitable when the text is taken out of context. He illustrated this in a humorous way on one occasion when he explained how he had been cured of juggling with the Bible. He flipped open the pages at random and ran his finger down the column. He found he was pointing to the story of Balaam and his ass. In another story he showed how by choosing isolated "proof texts" one can prove just about anything. He could prove that his audience should go out and hang themselves because Judas "went and hanged himself (Mt 27:5) and Luke 10:37 says, "Go, and do thou likewise."

A productive background was very much responsible for Morgan's well-developed gifts. At first glance one would not suspect such to be the case. He was born into the home of a little-known itinerant preacher, in a little-known place, Cutwell Villa, Tatbury, in Gloucestershire, England, in the year 1863. The beginning of his education was delayed because of poor health. At eight years of age, he suffered the loss of a sister who was dear to him. His teen years saw the end of his formal education.

Not very impressive on the surface, to say the least! But upon deeper investigation, the hand of Providence is evident indeed. When he was unable to attend school in his early years, an excellent tutor came to the Campbell home and grounded him in solid learning. His father's interest in preaching caught fire in the young boy's mind and heart, and the keen sense of loss in the death of his sister served to increase his native powers of sensitivity. Even as a boy, he was learning about self-examination and how to apply his insights to people in painful circumstances.

At thirteen he preached his first sermon, and at fifteen he commenced a preaching ministry here and there, wherever he could announce the good news.

No doubt the best-known formative event of his life was the questioning and searching period during the two or three years before his twenty-first birthday. Morgan, reflecting on this period, calls it the time his "early faith passed under eclipse." He quit preaching and refused even to open his Bible for two years, the "two years of sadness and sorrow." He tried one philosophy, then another. Finally, he took all his books, with their theories and notions, and locked them in a cupboard where he left them for seven years. Then he bought a new Bible and began to read it with an open mind and a determined will. The Book made his heart glow; the Word calmed his troubled intellect; the Scriptures gave him that "satisfaction that I had sought for elsewhere." From that time on, Morgan lived to preach the Bible.

Responsive people followed George Campbell Morgan. What a crowd gathered Sunday after Sunday at Westminster Chapel in London! People flocked to hear him from coast to coast in the States.

Wilbur M. Smith, well-known Bible teacher, testified that though he had been moved by many speakers, he knew of no one who could cast a spell over an audience like G. Campbell Morgan.

Perhaps John Henry Jowett discovered the key to Dr. Morgan's effectiveness when he noted that he let the Bible tell its own message. His genius for communicating that message was incomparable.

It was the "salty tang of freshness" and the "ringing tones of eternal truth" that brought people to Morgan. The sheer intensity of the man stimulated an already active mind and yielded a store of wisdom and knowledge that helped thousands.

In summary, it should be stressed that Dr. Morgan was an incessant, incisive, and careful student who was driven to preach his findings. He traveled widely to share his discoveries and learned to communicate with power. In this way, G. Campbell Morgan developed an enthusiastic, Word-oriented, and expectant following.

* * *

The Morgan literature is rich as resource material for the student of preaching. *The Analyzed Bible* (Westwood, N.J.: Revell, 1964) is an excellent start. *Preaching* (New York: Revell, 1937) is a valuable little book. For a study of his actual sermons, see the ten-volume *Westminster Pulpit* (New York: Revell, 1954).

Jill Morgan has done a biography called *A Man of the Word* (New York: Revell, 1951).

JOHN NEWTON
Warm-Hearted Preacher
1725-1807

John Newton

From an old print reprinted from *Tales of Grace* by C. Knapp (New York: Loizeaux, n.d.), facing page 32.

JOHN NEWTON

JOHN NEWTON was known as a forceful, energetic preacher who spoke from the pulpit with authority and prophetic urgency. People flocked to hear him because they got a message from God and caught his warm spirit. His manner was natural and unrehearsed; and though he prepared as faithfully as time permitted, he did not usually write out his sermons. "A word warm from the preacher's heart," he said, "is more likely to warm the hearts of the hearers." When the round of pastoral duties was too great to allow thorough preparation, he believed God would nonetheless take the preacher's humble words and use them to His glory. "Some person, whom you little think of, may have received conviction or comfort." "A whole sermon seldom gets through to people anyway; a detached sentence usually does the business."

Newton shaped his language and mood to the character of the ordinary audience. He learned how to do this by preaching to the poor people of Olney, a picturesque English town on the banks of the Ouse River. The chief industry was lace-making, and the townsfolk were uneducated and simple. But in these people he saw human nature react to the spiritual world and understood more about the work of grace and the wiles of Satan than he could have ever learned from a book. The faithful pastor, more frequently garbed in his sea jacket than his clericals, was constantly in and out of houses, drinking countless cups of tea, telling his tales from the days when he was a slave trader on the high seas. They loved him; he loved them. When in the pulpit, he talked their language and spoke to their problems.

Pastor Newton learned to speak to ordinary people also by working with the children of Olney. Many of them worked in the lace-making factories, too. They had their problems and knew what it was to be tired and sick of life. Yet there was a freshness in these small people. Newton caught their simple spirit and learned to communicate to them. "With them I was obliged to stoop in order to be understood; and I soon found that the familiar style I was obliged to use with children, was the most proper to engage the attention of grown people." His church in London was in the banking district, but he talked to the congregation there much as he did to the children in the rural church at Olney.

The love he had for children shone right through his person and preaching. People could tell that he possessed genuine concern. They knew him; they had watched him walk through the streets. Love for children breeds love for grown people, and love for both breeds power for communication.

Newton's background was checkered; he knew happiness and sadness, and had his ups and downs. As a child, he lost his mother. His father remarried, but John's new mother failed to treat him as her own son. At an early age, he quit school and went to sea. There he learned the rough ways of sailors; and though his real mother had taught him the Bible and the catechism, he soon gave up religion. In due course he became a slave trader and eventually captain of his own ship. Through the years, he picked up religion and set it down again several times. But one day, in a storm at sea that threatened his life, he surrendered to God in a new way. That story can be read in all its exciting detail in his spiritual autobiography, *The Authentic Narrative*.

The people of Olney "stare at me as I walk through the streets," he said, after the book had been published. And well they might look at him in awe and wonder! His preservation, both physical and spiritual, was evidence of Providence. It is no wonder that people listened to him. He once said that people came to see him as they do the lions at the Tower of London! He had been through a great deal.

But people came to him not only out of curiosity but for guidance and comfort as well. "I . . . heard a most touching sermon," a listener feelingly commented. "I never can forget the enjoyment and encouragement of the evening, or the delight of the whole church on that occasion."

Bernard Martin, author of *John Newton, a Biography*, estimates that Newton entered the pulpit ten thousand times in the course of his ministry. It may well be. He spoke from authentic experience, for he knew God in a real way. People want to hear a man with those qualifications. And people kept coming to hear him, even in the sunset years of his life. When he began to grow blind and deaf, he refused to give up preaching. His set of mind was unyielding surrender to Christ for ministry.

Richard Cecil once admonished him to stop preaching before he discovered he could speak no longer. The old gentleman's reply has echoed around the world: "I cannot stop. What! Shall the old African blasphemer stop while he can speak?" Newton's last service was in October, 1806. He preached a sermon honoring battle-scared heroes who had fought at Trafalgar. He went to his much deserved reward December 21, 1807, having run steadily the Christian race and having fought vigorously through the whole of his ministerial career.

Newton wrote his own epitaph, and that has become as famous as the African blasphemer quotation above.

JOHN NEWTON
Clerk,
Once an Infidel and Libertine
A Servant of Slaves in Africa,
was,
By the Rich Mercy of our Lord
and Saviour,
Jesus Christ
Preserved, Restored, Pardoned,
And Appointed to Preach the Faith
He had Long Laboured to Destroy.

He Ministered
Near XVI Years as Curate and Vicar
of Olney in Bucks,
And XXVIII as Rector
of These United Parishes.

On February the First MDCCL,
He Married
Mary,
Daughter of the Late George Catlett,
of Chatham, Kent,
Whom he Resigned
To the Lord Who Gave Her,
On December the XVth, MDCCXC.

* * *

Bernard Martin's *John Newton, a Biography* (London: William Heinemann, 1950) is available in America in paperback through Abingdon of Nashville, Tennessee. Newton's autobiography, *An Authentic Narrative,* has been published now and again through the years. Fourteen of his letters written about his experiences may be read in *John Newton: Out of the Depths* (Chicago: Moody, n.d.) .

PAUL STROMBERG REES

Disciplined Preacher

1900-

Paul Stromberg Rees
Courtesy of *The Herald*, Asbury Theological Seminary.

PAUL STROMBERG REES

It was a beautiful Kentucky afternoon in October. The colors of autumn were beginning to show above the perpetual green of the gently rolling hills of bluegrass. It was the kind of day that draws people outside—unless, of course, one is drawn inside to talk with someone extraordinarily interesting.

Paul Rees was that interesting someone. We took comfortable seats in the professor's den and began to talk. Delightful graciousness strikes one first of all. The love of Christ shines through Paul Rees; his eagerness to accommodate is very obvious and natural. This makes it easy to talk with him.

We talked about a subject as intriguing to preachers as any could be—homiletical method. Dr. Rees was kind enough to answer questions about his own method. Many of his comments had direct reference to his years in the pastorate. First, he shared this: that he kept a file of three-by-five-inch cards of potential sermon subjects. On them he recorded possible topics with texts, outlines, illustrations, and suggested bibliography. When ready to write a new sermon, he thumbed through his "jewel box," as he calls it, seeking a homiletical idea that would fire his imagination and meet the needs of his people for the particular occasion.

Once he had his idea, he proceeded to a fresh study of the chosen text within its context. That meant reading over and over again the literary unit of which the text was a part, which might be as much as a whole book of the Bible. The aim of this exercise was to get the actual, intended meaning of the text into the mind.

The next step was to examine the exegetical sources. Following that, the procedure was to discover how other preachers had treated the text. For this, expository homilies gave him more help than topical sermons.

As he did his "homework" step by step, Dr. Rees made notes under main headings. Illustrations and quotations he noted too, but used only those that had about them "the feeling of fitness."

Now began the process of typing out the notes and manuscript. While in the pastorate, he followed the practice of writing out full manuscripts for nearly every Sunday morning's sermon and most of the evening addresses. Because he was on the radio for the morning services, it was essential that quotations be given accurately, and to insure this, he read them directly from the manuscript. But he was in no sense glued to the papers before him; he had mastered the running discourse.

The two Sunday sermons took about thirty hours of specific preparation each week. Dr. Rees added that he is not a fast worker. At this point in the interview he gave a fitting quotation from his morning's reading: An author had been asked if he enjoyed writing. "No," replied the author, "I do not enjoy writing; I enjoy having written."

All this was very interesting, but I was curious about the resources that could make this kind of preaching possible Sunday after Sunday, year after year. Dr. Rees explained that in addition to his card file, he had spent a lifetime developing a letter-size file which today holds literally thousands of items, including poetry, clippings, historical information—anything at all that might assist in building solid sermons.

It is one thing to develop such a fine resource system, but quite another to employ it meaningfully. At this point he related with evident delight that his board at First Covenant Church of Minneapolis, where he was pastor for twenty years, had ordered him a workshop built in the daylight basement of the old church. They knocked out walls and had bookshelves installed for his extensive library.

"How many books do you have?" I interrupted.

"Fifteen thousand currently," he replied with a smile. "But don't forget that I had more than that in Minneapolis and have given away a good many since I left the pastorate some years ago."

By this time he was absorbed in reliving those days in the pastorate. He sat on the edge of his chair and gestured as he painted a word picture of his working situation. "I might have as many as forty books open at one time and be working on three or four projects. I might be at work on a sermon, an article, and a book all at once."

The picture was vivid and made me ask next about his reading habits.

"I have never taken a speed reading course. I read slowly. In fact, the more meaningful the book, the slower I read, because I like to underscore and write in the margins." To stop and ponder what he has read, to assimilate—that is his reading method.

His best reading is done early in the morning. Up at 4:30, never later than 5 A.M., he does his most creative work during the first hours of the day.

"How do you keep your health?" I queried.

"Well, I have no exercise program," he began, "but I have always walked a lot. I play golf every chance I get. In my younger days I played tennis."

"How many hours of sleep do you require?" seemed to come naturally at this point.

"I have always been quite fortunate. Five or five and a half hours is all I need." Then he added, "In the last few years, at my doctor's suggestion, I have been taking a fifteen minute nap in the middle of the day."

The sheer discipline of the man fascinated me. "My father was a strict disciplinarian," he commented. "He was an early riser."

Now the background of Paul Rees was coming to light, and

I ventured to ask more about his upbringing. In quick suc-
cession meaningful facts emerged. His father, Seth Rees, was
Welsh and preached with the eloquence and power of a
Welshman. On more than one occasion H. C. Morrison said
he was the most powerful preacher he had ever heard. His
father had bequeathed to Paul a deep and quiet prayer life,
too. Paul's mother, Frida Marie Stromberg Rees, was Swedish
and with Seth gave her son a reverential love for the Bible, a
love sustained throughout Dr. Rees' lifetime.

Comments on his youth led to asking when he preached his
first sermon. He was seventeen and delivered it at a downtown skid row mission in Los Angeles. With the preaching
of that first sermon came his first experience of the power of
the Holy Spirit in the spoken word, and also a profound peace
that the call he had been struggling with for some time was
authentic. He had wanted to be a lawyer or college professor,
either one; from that time he knew that he would be a minister of the gospel. The years have proved that his decision was
a sound one, for this man's preaching has touched thousands
around the world; and it has done so because he was first
touched by the Spirit of God.

The touch of the Spirit of God is the secret. The real motivation for building a great library, developing resource files,
doing painstaking manuscript work, maintaining careful dic-
tion and clear, forceful delivery is a profound sense of commission to bring the gospel to a lost and needy world.

*   *   *

Dr. Rees has published many books of sermons, such as *Things
Unsharable* (Grand Rapids: Eerdmans, 1948), which will chal-
lenge the preacher to sharpen his skills.

W. E. SANGSTER
Powerful Preacher
1900-1960

W. E. Sangster

From a photograph owned by Frank B. Stanger. Photograph by Henry James.

W. E. SANGSTER

W. E. SANGSTER couldn't keep his secret for preaching power! He gave it away without the slightest hesitancy in his book, *Power in Preaching*. It was his devout hope that many would follow his simple, workable seven-step formula:

1. Believe in preaching
2. Keep to centralities
3. Work at it
4. Make it plain
5. Make it practical
6. Glow over it
7. Steep it in prayer

There you have it! Now let's see how he put each step into practice.

Believe in it. If anyone believed in preaching, it was W. E. Sangster. No one could doubt his sincerity. Nor could anyone say he was lacking in conviction about the role of proclamation. He knew the power of the gospel and believed it without wavering. "No pulpit has power," he declared, "if it lacks deep faith in the message itself and in preaching as God's supreme method in making His message known."

If faith in preaching the gospel seems to be ebbing, Dr. Sangster advises one to nourish his faith in the gospel itself. Recall that the gospel cannot be known unless it is told, for people cannot think themselves into it. It is a revelation. "Grasp the fact that the heart of the gospel is a meeting of God and man, and preaching provides the best medium for that meeting." Also remember all that God has done through preaching in the past. Our civilization would not have survived until now without preaching. Finally, don't forget what preaching has done for you. Were you saved under it? Have you experienced healing through it? Sangster had.

Keep to centralities. No one can accuse W. E. Sangster of taking up precious preaching time with unproved positions or fringe issues. He believed that if the church could make some headway solving the real problems of our day, that in itself would be some accomplishment! This explains why he centered on the person and message of Jesus Christ. It also explains why he was a biblical preacher. He came right to grips with God and His power to save from sin, and he related these great truths to the concrete possibility of changed people and a reformed society.

The pulpit was no place for speculations and mere theories; it was God's ordained platform for the propagation of absolutely central and workable truth.

Work at it. What a worker at sermons was Dr. Sangster! After a full day of pastoral duties, he brought into the house an armload of heavy theological tomes over which he poured in order to get the rich background information for his sermons. A great amount of effort was given to the specific preparation of each sermon. He read his sermon manuscripts to his wife, who encouraged him to keep his preaching plain and simple. That leads to his fourth step.

Make it plain. Dr. Sangster stresses that a plumber must be able to understand your sermon. If anyone wants to think that you have no knowledge because you are easily understood or interesting to hear, let them think that. Sangster followed this guideline so that it was almost impossible to miss the meaning of a word in any of his written or spoken communications.

Make it practical. This does not mean that Sangster believed there was no place for the philosophical and apologetic type of preaching. He recognized that it could be of great service to nonbelievers and believers alike. He did not attempt to dismiss all questions from the pulpit, but he strove to select the right questions—the ones truly disturbing honest people.

Nor is it that all sermons must be ethical. There is, indeed, a place for ethical and devotional sermons in Dr. Sangster's scheme of preaching. He is keen on the theme of morality, but not to the exclusion of the atonement and the doctrines of Christian grace.

The point is that, whether a sermon is one of biblical interpretation, of ethics and devotion, doctrine, apologetics, social application, or evangelism, it must give directives for making life function better.

Glow over it. That is the same advice Pastor Sangster gives for repeating an old sermon. Can you glow over it? Does it excite you? Do you fire to it? Our people want us to get excited about our subject matter. More important, they know whether or not we have a message fresh from God. They can sense the preacher's intellectual and spiritual preparation, and they long to get a communication that is new and alive.

Sangster explains that, if the preacher's heart is thrilled and kindled, there is a good chance his people's hearts will be too. Just as fire spreads, a fiery message is contagious. It communicates.

If the preacher has prepared faithfully, he himself will be inspired. A sermon must be fresh and exciting to the preacher to be fresh and exciting to his congregation.

Steep it in prayer. A saintly minister once said that praying should be only one step beyond preaching. One must so bathe his message and himself in prayer that the actual delivery is praise to God; and when at last it is time for closing, the prayer will flow naturally out of the preaching just concluded.

Only the Spirit of God can communicate. Thus, we must commit the message to God, who takes it and drives it home.

Sangster points out the difference between preparing a sermon and preparing to preach. If one has been with God, people know it. If the minister is quiet and serene, confident in God and his message, people sense it intuitively. If the joy and excitement of God's presence is a reality to the preacher, it will be felt by the people.

* * *

Sangster shared widely his homiletical principles in *Power in Preaching* (Nashville, Tenn.: Abingdon, 1958) ; *The Craft of Sermon Construction* (Grand Rapids: Baker, 1972) ; *The Approach to Preaching* (Philadelphia: Westminster, 1952) ; and *The Craft of Sermon Illustration* (Philadelphia: Westminster, 1950) .

CHARLES HADDON SPURGEON

Gifted Preacher

1834-1892

Charles H. Spurgeon

From an engraving by F. T. Stuart, reprinted from *The Life and Labors of Charles H. Spurgeon* by Geo. C. Needham (Boston: Guernsey, 1881), frontispiece.

CHARLES HADDON SPURGEON

AT SIXTEEN YEARS OF AGE, Charles Spurgeon preached his first sermon. That was in the year 1850, and the place was a cottage at Teversham near Cambridge, England. He astonished his listeners with his oratorical powers, and from then on he was in demand as a speaker.

At eighteen he was invited to become the pastor of the Baptist congregation at Waterbeach, Cambridgeshire. Only two years later he began his London ministry, and within a year his once empty chapel, the New Park Street Church, was filled and overflowing. At twenty-two years of age he was the most popular preacher in London. A new building, the Metropolitan Tabernacle, had to be constructed to hold the crowds that came to hear the youthful prodigy with an amazing ability to capture and hold an audience.

Spurgeon came from Dutch heritage, his ancestors having migrated to England. In his family background were several generations of Free Church preachers. (The Free Churches in England are evangelical denominations independent of the established Church of England.) As a young boy he was employed by a Baptist. Spurgeon was converted in a Primitive Methodist Chapel. He became an active member of a Baptist Congregation in 1850, the year he preached his first sermon in the country cottage. So it was that Charles Spurgeon gave his life to the Free Church movement in England, and his tabernacle in London became one of the great Baptist centers of his age.

Spurgeon was independent in temperament. A law unto himself, he was bold, creative, utterly free, and capable of executing his ideas for the spread of the kingdom of God.

What ideas they were! The Metropolitan Tabernacle was itself a colossal undertaking. It seated six thousand, and he filled it consistently from 1861, the year of its completion, until his death in 1892. But while the Tabernacle was being built, he preached in the Surrey Gardens Music Hall to crowds of ten thousand. Once, on October 7, 1857, when he was but twenty-three years of age, he preached to twenty-four thousand in the Crystal Palace. It is estimated that in his thirty-four years of ministry he preached to ten million people.

While engaged in this demanding congregational ministry, Spurgeon carried on a variety of other ministries. He founded a pastor's college which became famous. Spurgeon's College has been responsible for training scores of evangelical workers. He established an orphanage for the care and education of destitute boys and girls that became a well-known philanthropy involving many in good deeds. He founded a colportage association whose employees were given a fixed salary in exchange for their whole time in literature distribution. Here was a noble attempt to lift the standard of reading material in a country plagued with unfit literature. From the year 1855, he produced a sermon a week for publication. His pen yielded an enormous amount of sermonic material. He may have written more printed sermons than any other man in church history. His monthly magazine, *Sword and Trowel*, enjoyed a wide and useful ministry. Wilbur M. Smith estimates that writings of Charles Spurgeon are equal in bulk to twenty-seven volumes of the ninth edition of the *Encyclopedia Britannica*. Moreover, his works have been translated into many languages, including Arabic, Armenian, Chinese, Congolese, Danish, Dutch, Estonian, Gaelic, German, and Spanish. In Germany, both during his lifetime and after, his works sold widely.

A further word about Spurgeon's printed ministry. Even though he produced a vast quantity of material, it was eminently worth reading. W. Robertson Nicoll, so long associated with the *British Weekly*, recommended reading in Spurgeon to be second only to the Bible in importance. Helmut Thielicke, the contemporary German preacher and theologian, has indicated his respect for Spurgeon in a work entitled, *Encounter With Spurgeon*. "Sell all that you have," he counsels the preacher, " (not least of all some of your stock of current sermonic literature) and buy Spurgeon (even if you have to grub through the second-hand bookstores) ."

Charles Spurgeon was a many-talented man. Energy, imagination, and authority were all his. Freedom and spontaneity characterized his speech. At the drop of a hat, he could make people laugh, and the freshness and insight with which he spoke made him absolutely fascinating.

Spurgeon's manner was quite unaffected. Plain and simple, he was distinctly countrified when he came to London to preach his trial sermons. Ernest Bacon provides a charming and colorful description of him arriving by the Eastern Counties Railway, getting off the train with his "rural clothes, large black satin stock, and a blue handerkerchief with white spots." That handerkerchief, says Mr. Bacon, was to get him into trouble, "for he flourished it vigorously during preaching—a habit they had not been accustomed to. The deacons tactfully gave him a dozen white handkerchiefs later." Something of this unvarnished and delightful unaffectedness no doubt stayed with him.

He was thoroughly grounded and secure in doctrine, and had the ability to make his beliefs contagious. These, coupled with his love for Jesus, contributed to the dynamics of his ministry.

Not only was Spurgeon well-informed biblically and doctrinally, but he was intensely aware of the contemporary scene and made shrewd comments on the behavior of his age.

Possessed of a thoroughly independent, strong personality, he was unafraid to fight for his convictions. His disagreements with his own Baptist association led to a schism in 1887 over what he called "slipping theology." He also withdrew from the Evangelical Alliance over baptismal regeneration.

Despite his individualism, Spurgeon was loved by large groups. In 1879, after completing twenty-five years at the Metropolitan Tabernacle, he was given a purse of 6,263 pounds as a symbol of the affection of the people.

Very importantly, Spurgeon was able to communicate his knowledge and his personality due to his mastery of public speaking. He spoke in a clear and natural voice and used easy and natural hand gestures. James Sheridan Knowles, an Irish dramatist and homiletician, called him "the most wonderful preacher in the world because of his perfection of oratory and his obvious acting abilities. . . . He can do anything he pleases with an audience!"

His knowledge of the Bible and a gift for unfolding its truths drew spiritually hungry people. Nearly fifteen thousand were added to his London church during the course of his ministry there.

In the final analysis, one must account for Charles Spurgeon's ministry in terms of the sovereign God. There is no other explanation for revival. Almost from his first Sunday in London, there was awakening; and it progressed steadily as souls found God in nearly every service. True, he had an especially good voice for public work; he was possessed of fiery passion; he was fluent; he had captured the secrets of sermon illustration. Yet, there is no way to explain a preaching and pastoral ministry like Spurgeon's except to say that it was a gift from God.

*   *   *

A biography referred to in this chapter is Ernest W. Bacon's *Spurgeon, Heir of the Puritans* (Grand Rapids: Eerdmans, 1968). Another recommended for further reading is W. Y. Fullerton's *Charles Haddon Spurgeon* (Chicago: Moody, 1966).

A compilation of his sermons, *The Treasury of Charles Spurgeon,* is in a paperback edition by Baker Book House of Grand Rapids, Michigan.

JAMES S. STEWART
Sensitive Preacher
1896-

James S. Stewart

JAMES S. STEWART

JAMES S. STEWART came to be known as "Stewart of Morning-side," pastor of Morningside Church, Edinburgh, from 1935 to 1946. The ushers of that church used to argue over who would be on duty for the night services. Each wanted to make sure that he had at least standing room to hear Dr. Stewart.

Hundreds of students who have read or listened to his sermons marvel at his brilliance. So distinguished is he among his colleagues that the General Assembly of the Church of Scotland named him as their moderator in 1963.

What is James Stewart's secret? Is it his scholarship? No one will deny him a solid place in the history of twentieth century religious scholarship. *A Man in Christ: The Vital Elements of St. Paul's Religion,* published in 1935, is the book that made him famous in the academic world. He contributed two volumes to the series called The Scholar as Preacher: *The Gates of the New Life* and *The Strong Name.* But his learning, as rich and significant for preaching as it is, is not the real secret of Stewart's prowess.

Is it his insight into homiletical theory? A more stirring document than *Heralds of God,* dealing with the method of the preacher, perhaps has not been produced in this century. Indeed, it is one of the few books, in the whole history of preaching theory, which is truly creative. Further, his Lyman Beecher lectures, *A Faith to Proclaim,* dealing with the content of preaching, is a magnificent volume, courageous and absolutely on target in its proclamations. His little booklet, *Exposition and Encounter,* the Joseph Smith Memorial lecture published in 1956, is in the same style as the two books just mentioned. There can be no doubt that Stewart has wrestled with the problems of pulpit communication and developed amazing skill. He is a great homiletician, yet there is more to the secret of his power.

There can be no doubt that the real key to Stewart's success is his sensitivity to human suffering which he believes only God can remedy. The note of pain is always in his preaching, for he knows and expresses with perfect accuracy the hurt of mankind. He makes one think, *That man puts into words just what I feel. He really knows my problems.*

Even a short sermon excerpt, taken from *The Strong Name*, reveals James Stewart's compassion. "There are so many forms of trouble in this world—physical, mental, emotional, spiritual. . . . One craves passionately to be able to let in some light upon the darkness, . . . the swift desolating calamities that crash their way through our hopes and dreams, all the slow, subtle disillusionments that steal the heart out of life. It is this aspect of experience, far more than any merely speculative doubt, which is the real threat to faith."

But, unlike so much modern preaching, his does not leave us struggling and agonizing with our doubts and problems; he shows the way to salvation. His formula is the New Testament one: The cross is followed by the resurrection; suffering then redemption; hurt then release; sin then forgiveness.

"Make us sons and daughters of the resurrection," he prayed. The sheer force and power of his voice and emphasis give only a glimpse of the spiritual power undergirding his utterance. This is the sum and substance of Stewart's preaching message. Stewart's great commission is to open the channels to the human heart so that those in need will respond to God's loving care.

One Saturday night before Easter, the guests in a hotel in the little country town of Kelso, Scotland, were seated about the fireside. A homemaker was knitting, her husband sat reading, a nurse busily wrote letters, and a minister was looking over the notes for his Sunday sermon. The radio was turned on, for Professor Stewart was about to preach over the

BBC. Only very shortly after he began, the housewife put down her knitting, her husband left his reading, the nurse looked up from her writing, and the minister put aside his preparation to listen to the imaginative and sympathetic voice which spoke of the resurrection of our Lord.

"Does Easter have a message for you?" he asked. "You have lost a loved one. Looking about you at the tragic state of the world, you have become disillusioned. Does the resurrection of Jesus Christ make any difference in such a world of suffering and misery?" The answer is intangible to the spiritually blind, but one wonders how long anyone could stay blind under such illuminating preaching. The resurrected Christ was shown as the answer to the difficulties of doubt, death, discouragement, and despair.

James Stewart possesses that prophetic power that tells the worshiper that God has spoken to him in need. The human and the divine have come together.

*　　*　　*

Stewart's books of sermons include *The Strong Name* (Edinburgh: T. & T. Clark, 1940), and *The Gates of the New Life* (Edinburgh: T. & T. Clark, 1937).

Heralds of God (New York: Scribner, 1946) is one of the great books on preaching of the century.

JOHN R. W. STOTT
Pastoral Preacher
1921-

John R. W. Stott
Courtesy of All Souls Church, London, England.

JOHN R. W. STOTT

A VISITOR to All Souls Church of Langham Place, London, is quickly made aware of the vital ministry of Pastor John R. W. Stott. He has oriented the people of his church in the heart of the city in four ways.

John Stott has emphasized that All Souls should be a prayer-oriented church. The first thing that impressed me as a visitor was the great congregation at prayer. An hour before the evening worship service, people were already in the sanctuary praying. More people joined them until the sanctuary, which holds about a thousand people, was fairly well filled by the opening of the service. It was rare for anyone to be seated without bowing his head in prayer. Even the young people were intent upon beginning the service in private prayer.

Think of a pastor receiving that kind of support! Any minister would preach better and do his pastoral work more efficiently with that kind of undergirding.

After the evening service there was a twenty minute informal prayer time by the baptismal font, the purpose of which was to dedicate the church's activities to God.

All Souls is also a person-oriented church. It is unusual to find a church so friendly. The members constitute a fellowship of concerned people, outgoing and pleasant to everyone who comes. The ushering system of All Souls is not the only factor that reflects this warm friendliness. Ushers were in the church early; one was there forty-five minutes ahead of time. The head usher was a very happy man who talked freely and unobtrusively to those he assisted.

There were many young people in the church—another evidence of a person-oriented community of believers. The leadership has worked out an excellent schedule of youth services. On Wednesdays, groups through the age of sixteen meet; and on Fridays, groups through the age of thirty. The youth are active, and the church provides facilities for their program. Latimer House, a center for young adults, constitutes part of those facilities. It occurred to me that the youth had something to draw them to this church—warm friendliness and the sense of belonging, coupled with the material necessities for an appealing program.

Other evidence that this is a person-oriented church is the marvelous way that everyone is included. A young boy brought the Bible to the reading desk before the beginning of the Sunday morning service and helped to arrange the choir chairs. There were many blacks and Indians in the church. A native African staff member who had helped in the Billy Graham campaign took part in the evening service. I noticed a poorly dressed man who sat in my row and a foreign-speaking girl who was given a good deal of attention by a girl friend with whom she apparently had come. The young, the dark-skinned, and the poor are all included with the hope that some may be won to Christ.

There is a welcome for children in the All Souls program, too. A nursery program is provided for those up to and through four years of age. For those older than four there is a service in an adjoining church building at 11:15 on Sunday morning. Parents are expected to attend with their children.

The intensive program of outreach which characterizes All Souls is impressive. There are luncheon addresses downtown in an honest attempt to reach business people. One Sunday, Pastor Stott spent a good deal of time announcing a service especially designed for the unconverted. Members were to offer tickets of admission to their neighbors. He explained that every Christian has a missionary obligation.

I thought, too, of the tremendous foreign missionary outreach of this church. One member is going overseas to work with spastic children. Making missions more real to the parishioners is a man from Uganda who serves on the staff.

Enough has been said to illustrate the fact that this is a person-oriented church. It is not a cold communion in which every man is left to shift for himself. Rather, the fellowship is characterized by warmth, and its reward is a hearty response.

All Souls is a literature-oriented church. In this day and age when so much attention is given to literature crusades of one kind or another, it is not surprising to see a thriving evangelical church give emphasis to literature. I stood in the foyer of All Souls and jotted down the titles of the books by Pastor Stott that were on sale: *Confess Your Sins; The Way of Reconciliation; Your Confirmation; Basic Christianity; The Preacher's Portrait; The Canticles and Selected Psalms* (one of a commentary series) ; *Inter-Communion and Prayerbook Revision; Personal Evangelism.* Pastor Stott has written other books as well. In addition, there is a substantial monthly church magazine which carries one of Stott's sermons.

Finally, All Souls is a preaching-oriented church. Dr. Stott's concept of the preacher's task is seen in his Fuller Theological Seminary lectures entitled, *The Preacher's Portrait.* He has a very specific idea of preaching, though one does not need to examine the book to learn what it is. Pastor Stott describes the true preacher as a specially called man who is God's instrument for communicating a message. It is the power of the Spirit that produces a true ministry. Stott is a strong believer in the literal power of the Holy Spirit.

On a Sunday morning following the closing of a Billy Graham crusade, an assistant at All Souls preached a simple gospel message which was aimed at helping those who had gone forward in the Graham meeting. It was a wholesome follow-up message. Stott's church had received two hundred commitment cards from the campaign. The simplicity, clarity, and biblical character of this follow-up sermon made it ideal for the occasion.

In the evening, Stott himself preached. He delivered a sermon which was part of a series on the book of Galatians. It was thoroughgoing biblical exposition—a type of preaching which we need more today but hear little of—and it was meaty and helpful. I was impressed with Stott's simplicity. Any ordinary man certainly could have understood his message.

Stott zeroed in on the necessity of the new birth. He showed the tendency to substitute an outward thing like baptism for the new birth. This, he observed, was the problem of the medieval church and the reason that the Reformation had come into being. This was also the problem of the eighteenth century church and the reason why Wesley and Whitefield had to be sent by God. There is no substitute for the new birth; true religion is inward, not outward. The cross is our provision for the new birth; but the natural man hates the cross because in it he sees himself a sinner, and no one likes what he sees when he looks into the mirror. Stott made the cross vivid.

In summary, a day at All Souls leaves a visitor impressed that here is a church that is warm and friendly, one to which he would like to return. Here is a church that has taken pains to provide physical facilities for carrying on a work of God. Here is a church that honors Spirit-filled preaching. Its ministry and the excellent response to it bear eloquent testimony to that fact. Here is a church that is carrying on a vigorous literature crusade. Books and magazine circulation prove that. All Souls is concerned about winning the lost. Its evident penetration demonstrates this fact. Here is a church spending much time talking to and listening to God. The picture of a great congregation at prayer is beautiful and deeply meaningful.

All this reflects the leadership of its pastor, Dr. John R. W. Stott, one of the great evangelical preachers of our day.

*   *   *

Stott gives us his perspective on biblical preaching in *The Preacher's Portrait* (Grand Rapids: Eerdmans, 1961) .

JOHN WESLEY
Persistent Preacher
1703-1791

John Wesley

From an oil painting by H. Goode at the John Wesley Seminary Foundation, Wilmore, Kentucky. Photograph by Henry James.

JOHN WESLEY

IN THIS CHAPTER John Wesley speaks for himself from his journal and letters on the subject of preaching. He lets us in on his views and convictions, and what he says is strangely alive, relevant, and meaningful for our own day. He also reveals the circumstances of his public ministry—sometimes difficult, nearly always rewarding. Whatever he tells us, we are informed and inspired.

Wesley advised young preachers to imitate St. John's simple style above all others. "Here are sublimity and simplicity together, the strongest sense and the plainest language!" Of Richard Bourke's preaching, he said he "united the wisdom and calmness of age with the simplicity of childhood." To Thomas Wride, Wesley wrote on May 5, 1790, "I hope you have *now* got quit of your queer, arch expressions in preaching, and that you speak as plain and dull as one of us."

Concerning content, Wesley wrote with a touch of humor: "My spirit was moved within me at the sermons I heard both morning and afternoon. They contained much truth, but were no more likely to awaken one soul than an Italian opera."

Evangelistic preaching must bring people to salvation. "I declared to about ten thousand, in Moorfields, what they must do to be saved." A frequently cited text was Mark 1:15: "The kingdom of God is at hand; repent ye, and believe the gospel." But John Wesley did not stop with initial salvation, he exhorted his people to go on to perfection: "I preached at four in the morning, on 'I am the Almighty God: walk before Me, and be thou perfect.'"

Wesley's pastoral heart shows up in his *Journal:* "I had a delightful opportunity in the evening of describing and comforting the 'broken in heart.' " But if he could comfort the sorrowing, he also could disturb the comfortable. In September of 1788, he wrote, "My Dear Brother,—It is certain you cannot preach the truth without offending those who preach the contrary. Nevertheless, you must preach it, only in the (most) inoffensive manner the thing will admit of." Then Wesley adds wise words of admonition: "And beware that you never return evil for evil . . . but contrariwise. . . . You cannot constrain any one to go to church; you can only advise them to it, and encourage them by example."

On one occasion he wrote, "Every time I preached I found more and more hope that God will revive His work in this city. I know He will, if the prayer meetings are restored; these are never without fruit." But prayer was no substitute for preaching. In his *Letters* we read, "I love prayer meetings and wish they were set up in every corner of the town. But I doubt whether it would be well to drop any of the times of preaching. Three-and-thirty years they have had at least as much preaching at Bristol as at Newcastle. And the congregations are far larger than they were ten or twenty years ago."

Wesley believed firmly in prayer for and the fact of divine healing, and experienced it on more than one occasion. Indeed there were times he could not have met his preaching appointments without a special act of God for his bodily health. His *Journal* entry for May 10, 1741, is thrilling. Part of it reads, "While I was speaking, my pain vanished, the fever left me, my bodily strength returned and for many weeks I felt neither weakness nor pain. 'Unto thee, O Lord, do I give thanks.' " The little English preacher learned the secret of strength. He had set out to preach on one occasion, he says in his *Journal,* but he was extremely weak and had been for days. "But God renewed my strength, so that I felt less pain and weariness every hour. I had a solemn and delightful ride to Keswick, having my mind stayed on God."

Wesley, strong or weak, well or ill, knew he must depend

on God: "I find it useful to be in . . . a state of suspense, wherein I know not what will be the next hour, but lean absolutely on His disposal, who knoweth and ruleth all things well." It is not surprising to see references to prayer and fasting in the *Journal* (cp. the journal of Francis Asbury) .

A letter of classic dimensions answers the question, Who is qualified to be a leader? "He must be a man of faith and love and one that has a single eye to the advancement of the kingdom of God. He must have a clear understanding; a ready utterance; diligence and activity, with a tolerable share of health. . . . He must likewise have some degree of learning; because there are many adversaries, learned as well as unlearned, whose mouths must be stopped. . . . Meet them on their own ground."

Constantly, Wesley pushed book circulation. He lamented the lack of books in his societies. Wesley himself was a great reader; for example, the *Journal* for October 13, 1752, indicates he had read Pascal's *Pensées*.

"I preached at Portarlington," he said in his *Journal* for August 28, 1752, "though I was extremely ill, and it was pain to me to speak; but it was a comfortable pain. I could from my heart praise God for His fatherly visitation." Nothing stopped him! "I preached in the evening, not far from the marketplace. There was a vast concourse of people, very few of the adult inhabitants of the town being wanting. I had gone through two-thirds of my discourse, to which the whole audience was deeply attentive when Mr. S—— sent his man to ride his horse to and fro through the midst of the congregation. Some of the chief men in the town bade me go on, and said no man should hinder me; but I judged it better to retire to the room. High and low, rich and poor, followed me; and soon filled, not only the room itself, but all the space near the doors and windows. God gave me, as it were, 'a sharp instrument, having teeth,' so that the stout-hearted trembled before Him. Oh the wisdom of God, in permitting Satan to drive all these people together into a place where nothing diverted their attention, but His word had its full force upon their hearts!"

Wherever there were people, John Wesley felt constrained to preach: "I bespoke the cabin in a ship bound for Dublin, which only waited for a wind." Status made no difference: "I preached in a large open space near the house, to many of the rich as well as poor." And he preached as often as he could to needy people: "I preached at five and at eight in Wednesbury; about one at Tipton Green; and at four in the afternoon to well nigh the whole town, high and low, as at the beginning." Nor did he preach more to the high than to the low. He showed his deep social concern in a *Journal* entry for October 2, 1739, where he laments that there is no worker with the "poor prisoners."

Anywhere, everywhere John Wesley and his preachers proclaimed the gospel: "It is a shame for any Methodist preacher to confine himself to one place. We are debtors to all the world. We are called to warn every one, to exhort every one, if by any means we may save some."

* * *

In addition to the eight-volume standard editions of Wesley's *Letters* (London: Epworth Press, 1931) and *The Journal of John Wesley, M.A.* (London: Robert Culley, 1909), there is an abridged paperback, edited by P. L. Parker, *The Journal of John Wesley* (Chicago: Moody, n.d.).

Arthur Skevington Wood's *The Burning Heart* (Grand Rapids: Eerdmans, 1967) is a first-rate source on Wesley's preaching.

GEORGE WHITEFIELD
Persuasive Preacher
1714-1770

George Whitefield

From the statue at the University of Pennsylvania. Courtesy of the University.

GEORGE WHITEFIELD

It is more than one man's opinion that George Whitefield was the greatest evangelist ever to come out of Britain, and certainly no one would deny him a high place in the history of preaching. His genius was his uncanny ability to persuade people. Once, Benjamin Franklin heard him speak. When Whitefield appealed for money, Franklin resolved that he would give him none. As the appeal continued, he decided he would give him his pennies. But Whitefield's oratory was so persuasive that next Franklin thought he should give his silver coins. By the time the collection plate was passed, however, Franklin was so moved that he contributed all he had in his pockets, even the gold coins.

Whitefield seems to have been born with the gift of persuasive speech. As a schoolboy, he would play truant for days to have time to prepare for plays he was to act in. But even though he was naturally gifted for public speaking, he put forth a great deal of effort to cultivate that gift. He studied oratorical techniques: the use of the voice, the role of gestures, the function of words. He mastered his art. And with his mastery came, in due course, a perfectly astonishing ability for extemporaneous speaking. With such ability, he was equipped to preach anywhere—at a college, under an elm tree, in a house, or in church. He was quite literally ready to preach at a moment's notice.

But it was not mere technique that made George Whitefield the persuasive speaker that he was. A deep and profound experience was the dynamic force in his ministry. It began back in his Oxford University days, when he and the Wesleys were members of the Holy Club. Charles Wesley loaned him

161

the book that was to be the means of his conversion, Henry Scougal's *The Life of God in the Soul of Man.*

Whitefield's call to preach was also part of a rich and growing experience with God. At first he believed he could not preach, but friends urged him and his convictions grew. The day prior to his ordination he spent in prayer and fasting. With the laying on of the bishop's hands, a spark was ignited in George Whitefield that was not to go out during his thirty-four years of preaching ministry. On both sides of the Atlantic he saw literally thousands come to hear the gospel. Countless men and women lighted their candles from his.

His voice was part of the secret of his persuasive power. He could be heard on clear days for a full mile. When Ben Franklin heard that Whitefield could make twenty-five thousand people hear him at one time, he didn't believe it until his own calculation convinced him that Whitefield could be heard by about thirty thousand. But it was not just volume that Whitefield had, it was his remarkable variety of tone— expressing at one time pathos; at another, joy; and at still another, judgment. Tenderness and sternness, love and anger—the whole gamut of emotions could be communicated through what must have been one of the most remarkable voices in speech history.

He put the whole man into his preaching. Gestures became a language supporting and emphasizing all that he said. His face was a veritable stage play of expression. Someone who heard him said it was "like a canvas and the preacher painted on it every passion that stirs in the human breast."

Whitefield's powers of description are famous. With word, heart, voice, and action, he drew pictures so vividly that listeners identified with the people and events being described. On one occasion, Whitefield was describing a blind beggar groping his way through a dark night near a precipice. The audience was so spellbound that they imagined they saw the poor man stumbling toward destruction. Lord Chesterfield, who was in the congregation, stood to his feet and cried out, "He is gone! He is gone!"

Still another factor that made Whitefield a master persuader was the frequency with which he preached. He believed that the best way to prepare to preach on Sunday was to preach every other day of the week.

But of more importance was his genuine concern for people. He almost never finished a sermon without tears, not tears of affectation but of sincere grief for the lost. It was obvious that his concern was born of God and that it was given in large measure.

To help people was the real motivation of this good man's heart. He studied with great care, mastering an English style which someone has termed "faultlessly easy." He possessed an in-depth knowledge of nature—all this to help people find God. His intense prayer life, learned early in his ministry, was motivated by his observation that the stronger he became inwardly, the more his outward sphere of action increased.

On more than one occasion, Whitefield expressed his profound concern for the lost. "God forbid that I should travel with anybody a quarter of an hour without speaking of Christ to them." He earnestly appealed to unbelievers, "Believe me, I am willing to go to prison and death for you. But I am not willing to go to heaven without you." Whittier the poet said of him,

> Up and down the world he went,
> A John the Baptist crying,
> "Repent!"

Someone who was fortunate enough to be close to him for a time observed that, "Day after day, from early morning, the house where the preacher entertained was besieged with weeping men and women, begging for a word of prayer and counsel, that they might find God."

Ebenezer Porter prepared a memorial inscription to Whitefield. It is an excellent summary of this great man's life and his power to persuade men to follow Christ: "The Rev. George Whitefield, born at Gloucester, England, December 16, 1714: educated at Oxford University: ordained 1736. In a ministry of thirty-four years he crossed the Atlantic thirteen times and preached more than eighteen thousand sermons. As a soldier of the cross—humble, devout, ardent—he put on the whole armor of God, preferring the honors of Christ to his own interest, repose, reputation, or life. As a Christian orator, his deep piety, disinterested zeal, and vivid imagination gave unexampled energy to his look, action, and utterance. Bold, fervent, pungent, and popular in his eloquence, no other uninspired (sic) man ever preached to so large assemblies, or enforced the simple truths of the gospel by motives so persuasive and awful, and with an influence so powerful on the hearts of his hearers. He died of asthma, September 30, 1770; suddenly exchanging his life of unparalleled labors for his eternal rest."

* * *

A life history of George Whitefield has been given us by Albert David Belden, entitled *George Whitefield—The Awakener: A Modern Study of the Evangelical Revival* (New York: Macmillan, 1953).

Also available is a compilation of his sermon outlines, edited by Sheldon B. Quincer: George Whitefield, *Sermon Outlines* (Grand Rapids: Eerdmans, 1956).

CONCLUSION
What Do Pulpit Giants Have in Common?

THERE ARE UNIVERSAL QUALITIES which characterize great preachers of any age. Those outstanding ones which mark pulpit giants of the past and present are the qualities which great preachers of the future will need in abundance in order to meet the challenges they will face.

Let us look at what pulpit giants have in common. There will be exceptions, of course, but the general characteristics of great preachers can be examined in the area of the spiritual and moral qualities of the preacher himself, the characteristics of great preaching, and the content or preachment which is notable in the ministries of great men of God.

THE PREACHER

Pulpit giants of the future, as those of the past, must take their call to preach with utmost seriousness. A sense of urgency is all important. This is exemplified by George Adam Clarke's ultimatum on the call: "Woe is me if I preach not the gospel."

Pulpit giants are possessed of a passion to communicate. Often they have it from childhood. There is within them an almost inborn drive which is certainly God-given. Spurgeon, the teenage orator, is a case in point.

Inevitably, they are individualists. Pulpit giants operate independently and unafraid. When opposed, they persist in following their God-ordained goals. Marshall's congregation criticized him, but he built a great ministry; Gossip's wife died unexpectedly, but domestic problems did not cut short a remarkable productivity; theories threatened Morgan, but by

165

faith built on experimental study, he articulated a great preaching principle, the contextual principle of Bible exposition.

All great preachers are eager students possessed of an insatiable desire to read and gather information. Adam Clarke is a case in point. Wesley insisted his preachers study several hours daily; of those who had no taste for study, he demanded that they develop it! From this fact comes a corollary: organized education holds considerable interest for great preachers. Wesley started the Kingswood school for boys, Spurgeon began a pastors' college, and John Newton wrote a plan for the training of clergymen.

All are writers. The alert preacher will be certain to print that literature from his ministry which can be of help to others. Wesley produced well over two hundred books; Luther has been called the Shakespeare of Germany; Rees keeps his pen meaningfully busy.

They are fervent evangelists; they must see people converted. They say with Richard Baxter, "I preach as a dying man to dying men."

The Holy Spirit overcomes weaknesses and handicaps, and develops the natural abilities of God's servants. Luther was intolerant, and Baxter was desperately ill; but their weaknesses were their strengths. Asbury possessed little formal training, and Bunyan was confined to prison; still they were marvelously used by God.

Numbers are comparatively unimportant. What happens to individual lives is all important. Each of the men in this book found themselves preaching to both large and small groups. Edwards preached to ordinary Sunday congregations and to revival crowds; Chadwick announced the good news to regular college chapels and to crowds so large that police had to be on hand; Asbury spoke for God in tiny house meetings and in great conferences. True effectiveness is determined by God, not by numbers.

Great men of God have an appreciation of nature. Edwards rode his horse; Moody was familiar with the shores of Lake Michigan; Stott leaves the city to be alone in the country. The heartbeat of God in the out-of-doors is heard through the stethoscope of the sensitive minister.

These men know continuing religious experiences. Pulpit giants know the meaning of "dying daily," "moving on" in the faith, growing in crises and from crisis to crisis. The ministry of F. B. Meyer illustrates this truth vividly.

Pulpit giants must be faithful men. Whether in sermon preparation or pastoral contact, in administration or fellowship, duty must not be neglected; indeed, one must go beyond duty. Compassion to help people in need caused Chadwick's faithfulness; a Spirit-led desire to build and rebuild lives kept Meyer faithful.

They are all busy men. Apparently the adage, "If you want to get something done, turn to a busy man," has achieved proverbial status with good reason. Effective preachers, such as Augustine in ancient times and Rees in our own time, have an enormous number of projects going at once; and apparently this extensive involvement in life is a factor in producing relevant material for the pulpit. Along with the multiplicity of effort is the capacity to concentrate meaningfully on one project at a time.

All memorable preachers are characterized by great joy. They are happy, excited people, filled with the joy of the Lord which is their strength. They have learned to look to the Lord and be radiant. Chadwick speaks of a "jolly" pastorate; Marshall loved a good party; Graham can make his people laugh. It is difficult to find a grouch or pessimist in the long line of historic greats.

Great preachers inevitably must struggle with success. They discover sooner or later that the ministry is not the glamorous business it appears to be from the outside, but it comes with enormous added responsibilities. Moreover, the successful preacher is never sure that he is successful. He sees so much more that needs to be done in the great enterprise of kingdom building. Wesley knew a continual holy discontent, and Sangster died full of ideas for kingdom advance.

Finally, pulpit giants are highly sensitive men. They feel deeply, hurt when others hurt, and sense what others may not sense. This heightened sensitivity promotes empathy and adds that difficult-to-define dimension to preaching that touches people precisely where they hurt.

THE PREACHING

Wit, humor, and logic tend to characterize the most communicable sermons. All three are interrelated. Wit is the capacity to make people laugh, often by clever expression or quick perception of the incongruous; humor is the ludicrous or absurd spoken in a comical mood; logic relates to a sequence of facts or events in an inevitable or predictable line, the opposite of the incongruous or the ludicrous. The wise preacher knows that he can communicate truth by reference to the humor of life's contradictions as well as to its normal and predictable situations. What a logician was Wesley! What a humorist Spurgeon was!

Each preacher must master his own method of delivery. Brooks read his sermons; Macartney insisted on preaching without notes; Whitefield could preach extemporaneously because he spoke several times a week, usually every day.

A preacher who has mastered the subject matter in order to produce a sermon manuscript will likely be capable of speaking from the overflow of a full heart. A. J. Gossip is a superb example. He wrote every sermon meticulously until he became an army chaplain. Then he no longer had leisure or place for manuscript work; but he discovered, much to his surprise, that he didn't need to write!

Simplicity characterizes great preaching. John Newton learned to preach to sophisticated London bankers by catechizing children of his Olney parish "in their own little way." In his work on homiletics, Augustine illustrated the dynamics of speaker-audience relationships from his own experiences of preaching to plain, unlettered people, yet his works still persuade the intellectual. Whether they spoke to ordinary or to learned people, great preachers kept their speech beautifully simple.

It is indeed rare to find a pulpit giant who is uninterested in music. The Wesleyan awakening established hymn-singing in the English-speaking world. Outstanding preachers have paid close attention to the role of music as a means of driving home the gospel message. The teamwork of Graham and Shea and of Moody and Sankey are well-known examples.

Wesley preached on a tombstone, in a field, in a doorway, in a garden, on a street, in a foundry. Clarence Edward Macartney had an outdoor pulpit. The burning heart of a great preacher reaches out for every opportunity to announce the good news, whether it be television, radio, Rotary Club, jail, a skid row mission, or a small gathering in a home.

The mechanics of speech—projection, articulation, gestures —are necessarily given attention by those who would be used of God as great preachers. John Wesley wrote *Directions Concerning Pronunciation and Gestures*; Spurgeon compiled a guide to pulpit work; Sangster produced a series of homiletical manuals. The great preachers oppose a stuffy preaching tone; they all possess that fearlessness that makes a man lift up his voice to declare God's good news with force.

Dull, cold preaching is forbidden. The writings of Baxter and Stewart contain eloquent passages on the warm heart and the quickened intellect. Dullness, says the pulpit giant, is inexcusable. Sangster enlivened his sermons by illustration and varied pace; Whitefield used vocal impression and facial expression.

Many notable men possess a lawyerlike capacity for argumentation and persuasion which they use for God. Finney was a lawyer; Edwards a logician. The good preacher has learned to employ argument as a means of persuasion with a skill similar to Paul's in Romans.

Successful pulpit men are at the same time truthful and tactful. Sentimentality must never be allowed to cover truth, yet bluntness must never deafen people to the truth. Bunyan, for instance, could say things in pictures which would have been quite unacceptable in a different verbal setting.

The preacher with the telling message speaks with originality and freshness. He does not use originality for originality's sake but as an instrument of gospel communication. The Spirit uses the raw materials of a man's life, the creative impulses of his unique mind, and the rich images of his sanctified imagination. Note the creativity of Sangster, Stott, and Stewart. One clue is, of course, the constant collecting and filing of ideas and illustrations which assist greatly in the production of a constant flow of fresh sermonic materials.

THE PREACHMENT

G. Campbell Morgan and John R. W. Stott typify the authentic preacher's aim to communicate Bible-based truth with sufficient power to make it stick and to get people to act upon it. The Scriptures must be preached, and they must be preached with power.

All pulpit giants understand the human heart. John Newton said there are three books the preacher must learn: the Bible, the book of nature, and the book of the human heart. The latter book is learned often through suffering, thus Bunyan the prisoner can speak with an almost uncanny clarity about human nature.

Great preaching is inevitably related to teaching. In classroom language, *kerygma* and *didache* find their way into the preacher's communication. This is the New Testament pattern: proclamation of the gospel to the unconverted and the nurturing of the converted in the faith. Reformers like Luther were masters at both, and this accounts in a very important way for their success.

While each preacher tends to have his own emphasis, such as Billy Graham's stress on decision, the whole gospel must be preached, including both grace and judgment. It is rare to find an effective preacher with a one-sided emphasis.

Notable preachers in every age have the capacity to catch the moods and needs of their time and situation. Brooks could communicate to the university student and to the sophisticated Bostonian. Wesley spoke a morally reforming word in a thoroughly corrupt age.

The alert and effective preacher has learned to think homiletically. Mundane experiences can become lively illustrations for the gifted preacher. What may be a dull outline can become a gripping sermon structure with the deft changes of the homiletician. Everything is potential material for proclamation. Macartney took three obscure words from Paul, "come before winter," and made of them an evangelistic sermon which he preached annually to hundreds.

Universally, prayer is undeniably a fundamental requirement in the making of both preacher and preachment. Prophetic communicators get their sermons on their knees. Rees learned to pray at his father's side and at his mother's knee; Meyer was a man of great devotional depth; Moody knew from personal experience the value of a prayer meeting. If a message is to carry the Word of God, it must come from God who enlivens the words.

Great preaching inevitably has its social outreach. Whitefield began an orphanage; Finney founded a college; Spurgeon started a colportage association. This is the Christian message with feet to it!

It is important that the Old and New Testaments be expounded in balance. The Old is seen as preparation for the New. The Old emphasizes law, while the New highlights grace. Moody and Newton showed this balance, for they were as at home with the Old Testament figures as they were with Jesus and Paul.

Notice, too, that each pulpit giant thinks of preaching as the most important activity in which he participates. In preaching, God literally communicates His Word. Thus James S. Stewart can say that every Sunday morning the true preacher believes that, "God is to be in action today, through me, for these people. This day may be crucial, this service decisive, for someone now ripe for the vision of Jesus."

It is appropriate to conclude with the fact that pulpit giants have a burning within their souls to see renewal. The pulpit pleas of Baxter and the private prayers of Finney are reflections of that fire. To witness the church and its members actually awakened and sent into a diseased world to heal it, would be the fulfillment of the highest dream of any Spirit-dominated preacher.

*   *   *

What will characterize the pulpit giants of tomorrow? Clearly, there can be no mouthpiece for God, no authentic prophet, without very special gifts to cope with the unique problems of the times. The need is critical, and there is little doubt of the uniqueness of today's crises.

What other age has so deliberately rejected history with all its lessons? What other age has embraced such a widespread Phoenix mentality that says, "Destroy! Burn! Out of the ashes will rise something new"? What other age has struggled with such personal meaninglessness and has been so immoral —not only sexually but ethically in every regard? Has any other age suffered such irreconcilable gaps between old and young, specialists and generalists, cultured and unrefined?

First, the budding preachers of today, in order to become the pulpit giants of tomorrow, must have that special touch by the Holy Spirit which sets them apart as ministers with talents tailored to meet the crises of our times. They must be chosen by God for this purpose.

Second, they must develop a holy toughness. An age as sinful as ours resists the gospel with all its might. It cries out against the very foundations of righteousness. This kind of reaction is already familiar to us in the "God is dead" movement, which started in the church itself. Further evidence of decay in the church is its laissez-faire attitude toward sexual morality. (In a recent survey, 76 percent of boys from evangelical churches had had sexual experience after "conversion"!). Tomorrow's pulpits will require independent, tough-minded men of steel who can and will preach against sin. Such pulpit giants will stand out in stark contrast to the typically and ethically spineless person characteristic of our society.

Today is not a time for indecisive, ineffectual Christian workers. Iron men are needed. And though there will be those ready to fight against such men with both obvious and subtle weapons, there also will be those ready to support the noble and the righteous.

Third, they must couple a divine tenderness with that toughness. Sin makes the preacher angry. He cries out against it with all the eloquence at his command. It also makes him weep as he pleads with the heartfelt concern of Jesus for the salvation of the lost and the reformation of wrongdoers. Thus, when he preaches with Billy Sunday fervor against evil, his words and the very tone of his voice bespeak a pathos that communicates an honest and profound love.

Someone has called this coupling of toughness and tenderness a steel-and-velvet characteristic. Here is no mere sentimentality, but divine firmness. It is the roar of a lion protecting her cubs; it is the discipline of a judge restraining a youth from the clutches of a horrid future.

Fourth, they need to be tutored in skills and knowledge essential for proclamation of God's message. Foundational is the use and interpretation of the Bible. They will know how to apply the Word that wounds the frivolous and heals the fainting in the continuous battle of the Word against the world. They will apply that Word to themselves as well, weaving the spirit and eternal meaning of the Word into the fabric of their life styles and world views.

In order to communicate that Word effectively, the preacher will need to know the psychology of speech and public proclamation, and the techniques which make for power in presentation.

The pulpit giants of tomorrow will be those specially *touched* by the Holy Spirit, *toughened* and made *tender* by Him, and *tutored* in skills and knowledge essential for proclamation.

Finally, he will be a man skilled in effective contact with God. If the saints and preachers of the ages have known that there is no effectual preaching without prayer, the sermonizer of tomorrow will know that he is absolutely destitute without it. He will discover, as comparatively few in the past have, that the powerful preacher is made in prayer. Thus God will provide subjects and content for times and seasons, using His chosen and prepared vessel to deliver the message to those to whom he is sent.